ARTS & CRAFTS

HOME PLANS

hanley wood
HomePlanners

SHOWCASING 85 HOME PLANS
IN THE CRAFTSMAN, PRAIRIE, AND BUNGALOW STYLES

ARTS & CRAFTS
HOME PLANS

PUBLISHED BY HOME PLANNERS, LLC
WHOLLY OWNED BY HANLEY-WOOD, LLC

President, Jayne Fenton
Chief Financial Officer, Joe Carroll
Vice President, Publishing, Jennifer Pearce
Vice President, General Manager, Marc Wheeler
Executive Editor, Linda Bellamy
National Sales Manager, Book Division, Julie Marshall
Managing Editor, Jason D. Vaughan
Special Projects Editor, Kristin Schneidler
Editor, Nate Ewell
Lead Plans Associate, Morenci C. Clark
Plans Associates, Elizabeth Landry, Nick Nieskes
Proofreaders/Copywriters, Douglas Jenness
Technical Specialist, Jay C. Walsh
Lead Data Coordinator, Fran Altemose
Data Coordinators, Misty Boler, Melissa Siewert
Production Director, Sara Lisa
Production Manager, Brenda McClary

BIG DESIGNS, INC.
President, Creative Director, Anthony D'Elia
Vice President, Business Manager, Megan D'Elia
Vice President, Design Director, Chris Bonavita
Editorial Director, John Roach
Assistant Editor, Tricia Starkey
Director of Design and Production, Stephen Reinfurt
Group Art Director, Kevin Limongelli
Photo Editor, Christine DiVuolo
Art Director, Jessica Hagenbuch
Graphic Designer, Mary Ellen Mulshine
Graphic Designer, Lindsey O'Neill-Myers
Graphic Designer, Jacque Young
Assistant Photo Editor, Brian Wilson
Project Director, David Barbella
Assistant Production Manager, Rich Fuentes

PHOTO CREDITS
Front Cover and Title Page: Design HPT9900003; for details see page 33. Photo by Northlight Photography.
Facing page, left: Design HPT9900009; for details see page 24. Photo by David Papazian.
Facing page, right: Design HPT9900001; for details, see page 28. Photo courtesy of Roger Wade Studios, Inc.
Back Cover, Top: Design HPT9900002; for details see page 24. Photo by David Papazian.
Back Cover, Bottom: Design HPT9900001; for details, see page 28. Photo courtesy of Roger Wade Studios, Inc.

Hanley Wood HomePlanners Corporate Office
3275 W. Ina Road, Suite 220
Tucson, Arizona 85741

Distribution Center
29333 Lorie Lane
Wixom, Michigan 48393

© 2004

10 9 8 7 6 5 4 3 2 1

Printed in the United States of America

Library of Congress Catalog Control Number: 2003113858

ISBN 1-931131-26-0

ARTS & CRAFTS
HOME PLANS

CONTENTS

FROM MAGNIFICENCE TO MODESTY: THE ARTS & CRAFTS MOVEMENT

Reacting against the opulence of the Victorian era, Arts & Crafts proponents called for a return to simpler times

The Arts & Crafts movement, which began in mid-19th century England, was inspired by the opulent exteriors and interiors of middle-class Victorian-era homes. These homes often included formal rooms—parlors, dining rooms, and drawing rooms—and featured interiors with bright, floral-patterned wallpaper; large pieces of furniture made of dark woods and complemented by rich red and gold shades; lacy curtains and doilies; and heavy or fringed draperies. Small ornamental objects, many of them reproductions, were found everywhere. But due to the Industrial Revolution, many of the decorative objects that filled Victorian homes were mass-produced by machines—and early Arts & Crafts figures like William Morris, John Ruskin, and August Pugin began advocating a return to simpler, handmade items, designed and produced by skilled craftsmen.

In England, the Arts & Crafts movement focused on reviving Gothic and medieval styles; the idea of craftsmens' guilds, which existed during the Middle Ages, was particularly appealing to movement leaders. But this led to the Arts & Crafts movement being confined to the upper classes: the refusal to rely on machines created the need to pay skilled craftsmen, and the working classes could not afford craftsmens' prices.

In America, however, the Arts & Crafts philosophies were adapted a bit, and the movement enjoyed a wider audience. American designers found inspiration in nature and its materials—wood, stone, clay, and metal. Interior woodwork, arranged to best showcase the grain of the

ABOVE AND OPPOSITE PAGE: Arts & Crafts designs highlighted interior woodwork and relied on subtle, earth-toned shades. RIGHT TOP AND BOTTOM: Bright colors, lacy draperies and intricate woodwork, similar to those in these modern examples, filled Victorian-era interiors.

wood, was common in American Arts & Crafts homes; so were earth-toned paints and simple yet elegant pottery. And, although furniture was often hand-finished by craftsmen, it was produced by machines, thereby lowering the cost and making the furnishings more affordable.

The American Arts & Crafts movement inspired several distinct architecture styles—Craftsman, Bungalow, and Prairie—and generated a variety of furnishings, with uncomplicated patterns and simple lines, that is still popular today. Turn the page to learn about each design style, and begin your own Arts & Crafts revival. ■

CRAFTSMAN STYLE

Clean, simple lines and regional materials allow Craftsman-style plans to blend seamlessly with the landscapes that surround them

The Palladian window receives a Craftsman treatment for this design. For details, see page 69.

Craftsman architecture, design, and furnishings swept the nation in the late 1890s, reaching the height of their popularity between 1905 and 1920. Gustav Stickley, a young furniture maker from New York, defined this American interpretation of Arts & Crafts style. Inspired by British Arts & Crafts leaders John Ruskin and William Morris during an 1897 trip to England, Stickley decided to create a new line of handcrafted furniture, and introduced the Craftsman line in 1898. In 1901, to share his ideas about architecture and design as well as furniture-making, he began publishing a magazine called *The Craftsman*. Early issues focused on furniture and architectural details, and soon each issue featured at least one house plan. These designs included floor plans and were often

This charming plan displays the low-pitched roof, gable detailing, and sturdy porch columns of Craftsman style. For a similar plan, see page 76.

American Craftsman design
was partially inspired
by Asian style elements,
like the low-pitched roof of
this Japanese house.

presented with extensive details such as interior renderings, woodwork designs, and color combinations, paint, rugs, and curtains. Plans could be purchased through the magazine, and Stickley sold all of the interior accessories through his furniture catalogs. In 1907, Stickley stopped publishing house plans for a brief period to concentrate on establishing his

own Craftsman home (today called Craftsman Farms), but resumed in 1908. By this time, the house plans featured interiors designed around fireplaces—Stickley's idea about a gathering area with a fireplace serving as a center of family activity has proven to be timeless, with many of today's floor plans revolving around a great room with a

This two-story home features a hipped roof instead of the more typical gabled roof, but retains the decorative supports, stone accents, and wide porch columns. For details, see page 79.

CRAFTSMAN STYLE ELEMENTS:

- Low-pitched, gabled roof with a wide overhang and exposed rafters
- Decorative beams under gables
- Facade usually composed of regional materials: clapboard or shingle siding, with stone accents
- Square porch columns that extend to ground level
- Distinctive windows: multipane on top, single-pane on bottom
- Interior woodwork
- Fireplaces that serve as focal points of a gathering area
- Built-in benches, cabinets, and shelves that maximize interior space

This modern plan showcases all of the elements of Craftsman style: low-pitched, beamed gables, detailed windows, porch columns that extend to ground level, and a siding facade with stone accents. For details, see page 54.

central fireplace. More than 220 house designs were published in The Craftsman before publication ceased in 1916.

Craftsman homes have a variety of elements in common. Most feature low-pitched, sloping rooflines with wide eave overhangs; these rooflines were inspired by the simple yet beautiful architecture of Asia. And, unlike many Victorian-style homes, which featured decorative millwork, Craftsman homes were unadorned, relying instead on exposed structural elements—gable beams and rafter tails—to add visual appeal. (Furniture produced by Stickley was also well known for this.) Craftsman homes were meant to exist in harmony with the landscapes that surrounded them, so

they were composed of natural materials—clapboard siding, cedar shingles, stone, and even logs. (The main dwelling at Craftsman Farms, originally meant to be a school for boys but eventually used as the Stickley family home, was a large log house.) Floor plans were open, and to maximize the living spaces, Stickely advocated the use of built-in bookshelves, benches, and cabinetry.

True "Craftsman" homes are limited to those plans published in Stickley's magazine, but plenty of other architects and designers of the period adapted Arts & Crafts elements to create their own Craftsman-inspired designs. For a portfolio of modern homes with Craftsman influences, turn to page 33. ■

BUNGALOW STYLE

Practical, versatile, and entirely comfortable, the bungalow style holds a timeless appeal

This bungalow, with its stone-and-shingle facade, honors the tradition of building with natural materials. For details, see page 95.

The bungalow is one of the most popular and enduring styles in American architecture—and this is because, in part, the term "bungalow" is very general and can apply to many different housing styles! According to *American Bungalow* magazine, nearly every type of house has been called a bungalow—there have been shingle-style bungalows, Folk Victorian bungalows, and even Spanish Colonial bungalows. And it's easy to see why; the Merriam-Webster dictionary defines a bungalow as "a usually one-storied house with a low-pitched roof," and one-story houses can be found in any style. And, to add to the confusion, the Gamble House—the best-known example of Charles & Henry Greene's work and considered one of their "ultimate bungalow" plans—is an expansive two-story home. But the word "bungalow" has its roots in India, where native dwellings were called "bangala." These simple—and one-story—huts were adapted by British

A wide, welcoming front porch highlights this shingled bungalow. RIGHT: A clapboard exterior and standing-seam roof give this bungalow a breezy air, making it suitable for a waterfront retreat. For details, see page 94. For a similar home, see page 100.

OPPOSITE: ©ROB MELNYCHUK/GETTY IMAGES; RIGHT:

THE BUNGALOW STORY

Bungalows:

■ were inspired by *bangala*, native dwellings in India, and adapted by British colonists.
■ are usually one-story or one-and-a-half-story, although there are historic examples of two-story bungalows.
■ were popular with the American middle and working classes during the years between 1880 and 1930.
■ often incorporate elements of Craftsman style, both inside and outside.
■ were initially marketed as carefree, comfortable vacation homes—perfect retreats for hardworking American families.
■ became so prevalent that they ended up being the most popular home for hardworking American families.

colonists to feature central gathering rooms surrounded by bedrooms, bathrooms, and other living spaces. Bungalows suited the Arts & Crafts era well; their uncomplicated layouts and reliance on regional building materials blended well with the movement's ideals.

Bungalows are often associated with Craftsman-style homes, largely because their periods of popularity coincided; most American bungalows were built between 1880 and 1930. Many bungalows share the low-pitched roof and sturdy porch pillars of Craftsman style, and some even include the distinctive window designs and interior woodwork detailing. The first American bungalows were built

RIGHT AND BELOW:
These two charming
stucco bungalows,
which would look
right at home
in warm Western
climates, boast
Craftsman details like
exposed rafter tails
and pillared porches.
For details, see
pages 102 and 89.

on the East Coast, but the style quickly spread to the West as well; Americans would often move westward for health or economic reasons, and bungalows were an affordable housing option that conveyed a comfortable, carefree lifestyle. In fact, the rise of the bungalow can be credited in large part to middle- and working-class Americans; the wealthy could build Arts & Crafts homes by securing the services of architects like the Greene brothers or Frank Lloyd Wright, but the working classes, unable to build custom homes, turned to pre-designed bungalows.

The demand for bungalows was answered by a variety of mail-order companies; two of the better-known companies were Sears, Roebuck and Company and the Aladdin Company. In the years between 1908 and 1940, Sears ran a mail-order homes division, which shipped house plans and the materials needed to build them to all areas of the United States. Some of their best-selling designs were bungalows. The Aladdin Company was founded in 1906, and by 1917, the company was selling more than 3,000 bungalow plans each year. Both Sears and the Aladdin Company initially portrayed bungalows as vacation retreats—places where hardworking people could escape from their worries—but the style became so popular that the bungalow style was prevalent in many suburbs.

The bungalow plans collected in *Arts & Crafts Home Plans* are inspired by the Craftsman-style bungalows of the Arts & Crafts period. Some, like the home on page 80, could serve as vacation retreats; others, like the design on page 84, would look right at home in today's subdivisions. And, in honor of the Greene brothers, we've even included some two-story homes. To browse through the Bungalow section, turn to page 80. ∎

AMERICAN FOURSQUARE AND PRAIRIE STYLE

Beautiful in their simplicity, the Foursquare and
Prairie styles are at home anywhere

With a massive central chimney, windows both large and small, and a low-slung hipped roof, this plan exemplifies Prairie style. For details, see page 114.

American architect Frank Lloyd Wright, born in 1867, was one of the first to create a truly American form of architecture. In 1887, Wright began his career in Chicago; by 1897, he had joined other architects of the day in casting off the opulent designs of the Victorian era and adopting the ideals of the Arts & Crafts movement. Wright believed in "organic" architecture: he thought that homes should appear to grow from their sites, just as plants grew from soil. Like those who designed Craftsman-style and bungalow homes, he felt that a large gathering room with a fireplace should serve as the center of family life, and that the remaining

rooms should be as simple and open as possible.

American Foursquare homes, today considered a subtype of the Prairie style, included some of the features that would later define Prairie-style architecture; sometimes they are called "Prairie Boxes." Their simple, boxy shape served a dual purpose, allowing them to fit easily on city lots and permitting larger interior rooms. Foursquare homes were usually two or two-and-a-half stories high, with low-pitched, hipped rooflines; full-width front porches, and a central dormer window, also with a hipped roof. Like bungalows, foursquare

plans offered central fireplaces and plenty of built-ins; they were also sold through mail-order catalogs and pattern books. Foursquare homes were popular in the years between 1895 and 1930.

In 1901, a plan designed by Frank Lloyd Wright appeared in *Ladies Home*

PRAIRIE STYLE AT A GLANCE

- Low-pitched roof with wide overhanging eaves
- Open floor plan, sometimes with glass panels separating rooms instead of walls
- Combination of one- and two-story wings
- Massive central chimney
- Ribbons of small windows
- Emphasis on horizontal lines

The Taliesin estate, Frank Lloyd Wright's home for 48 years, covers 600 acres.

This modern design embodies all of the main American Foursquare characteristics: a large central dormer window, a full-width front porch, a hipped roof, and a boxy, symmetrical facade. For details, see page 109.

FOURSQUARE FEATURES

- Simple, boxy shape suited to city lots
- Two or two-and-a-half stories
- Low-pitched, hipped roof
- Single central dormer window
- Covered front porch that spans width of home
- Usually symmetrical facade (some examples feature an off-center entrance).

Journal; the article was called "A Home in a Prairie Town," and from then on, this distinctive style was known as the Prairie Style. These plans were designed to complement the flat, rolling terrain of Wright's native Midwestern prairies. By using horizontal lines, low-pitched rooflines, and sturdy porch supports, the designs both rose above the prairie and were anchored to it. Prairie designs were usually a mix of one- and two-story wings, and featured a large central chimney. Interiors were open and flowing; often, rooms were not separated by walls but by movable partitions or leaded glass panels, which allowed the central fireplace to warm the entire home.

Prairie-style homes enjoyed popularity between 1900 and 1920; after that, they were eclipsed by the post-World War I trend of styles like Early American and Colonial Revival. Today, examples of this style can be found mainly throughout the Midwest, where the designs were most common. To view some modern Prairie- and American Foursquare-style plans, turn to page 106. ∎

ABOVE: The entry of this traditional home provides an introduction to its textured walls and plentiful interior woodwork. Interior design by The Craftsman Home (www.thecraftsmanhome.com). LEFT: The Arts and Crafts interior of Little Holland House, designed and built by Frank Dickinson.

ARTS & CRAFTS INTERIORS

Like the simple, harmonious exteriors of the era, Arts & Crafts interiors relied on earth tones and natural materials

Harmony and simplicity were the defining characteristics of Arts & Crafts-style interiors, and the three most common American styles of the period—Craftsman, Prairie, and Bungalow—featured some of the same elements. All three styles revolved around one main interior living space, usually a great room with a central fireplace; in the purest Prairie-style homes, the entire living space was one large area, with screens or leaded-glass panels providing divisions between rooms. Decorative fabrics, like the heavy curtains of Victorian-style interiors, were uncommon; instead, the windows themselves were decorated, often with geometric stained-glass patterns. The theme of using natural materials on exteriors was echoed inside; Craftsman-style homes and bungalows both featured a great deal of interior woodwork, including flooring, beamed ceilings, and paneled walls. Tables and chairs were built with clean, straight lines

INTERIORS

and unadorned woods, and a common centerpiece to the living area was the settle, a long, bench-like piece that was covered with upholstered or leather cushions and used as a sofa. (These settles were inspired by medieval benches, which required high backs to protect people from cold drafts—to honor their medieval roots, settles were often high-backed, and so were many Arts & Crafts-style chairs.) The Arts & Crafts era also encouraged natural lighting whenever possible, and a wide variety of distinctive lamps provided additional illumination. Earth tones—for paint,

RIGHT: This high-backed chair displays the clean, simple lines of the Arts & Crafts style. BELOW: The main living room of the all-redwood, Craftsman-style, Harbor House Inn is still in its original state and features the Mullgardt fireplace at the center of the room.

ABOVE: A home on South Carolina's Spring Island features Arts & Crafts details in the great room. Cherry wood floors, a vaulted ceiling, and a large stone fireplace are a backdrop to Thomas Moser furniture.
LEFT: The parlor of this California home boasts textured walls and a richly colored rug. Interior design by The Craftsman Home (www.thecraftsmanhome.com).

wallpaper, and rugs, were popular, and wallpaper and rug patterns usually revolved around nature—birds, flowers, and leaves. And ornamental objects—though minimal—were present, usually consisting of carefully selected pottery or metalwork. Arts & Crafts pottery, like wallpaper, incorporated natural themes—birds, flowers, and animals—and copper, brass, and pewter, with their rustic appeal, were fashionable metals.

Turn the pages to find examples of Arts & Crafts interiors—some are historic and some are modern, but all promote harmony and simplicity. ∎

This traditional home in Piedmont, California, features interior design by The Craftsman Home (www.thecraftsmanhome.com). Note the wood paneling and floors, the simple yet elegant settle, and the built-in cabinetry that surrounds the fireplace.

RIGHT: The foyer boasts lovely display cabinets, a built-in bench, and a hardwood floor with unique detailing. OPPOSITE PAGE: Stone accents and window detailing highlight the home's exterior.

CRAFTSMAN CLASSIC

Rafter tails, gabled rooflines, and sturdy stone pillars enhance an Arts & Crafts home with a sense of history

This splendid version of Craftsman style is well suited to any neighborhood, whether it's an Arcadian suburb or the heart of the country. The covered front porch, complete with built-in benches, opens to a grand foyer. Defined by crafted columns, this elaborate space provides a coat closet and a wide bench framed by cabinets. French doors lead to a private study, which features a window seat, built-in bookshelves, and a plate shelf that sur-

rounds the room. A fireplace will warm cool evenings and cozy gatherings, and plenty of windows and a French door to a secluded deck provide natural light.

The foyer opens to a formal dining room through a banquet of decorative columns; this elegant space features a beamed ceiling and a built-in hutch with recessed lighting, enhanced by a stunning triple window. Just steps away is the spacious, well-planned kitchen, which boasts wood cabinetry and

PHOTOGRAPHY BY DAVID PAPAZIAN

A window seat and built-in bookshelves highlight this corner of the study.

ABOVE: A fireplace with a tile surround is the focal point of the study, where understated yet rich colors hold sway.

hardwood floors. A hanging pan rack, both decorative and useful, crowns the central work island. A built-in planning desk complements wrapping counter space and plenty of drawers and cabinets. The family cook will appreciate the walk-in pantry, vegetable sink, and six-burner stovetop. A counter with a double sink overlooks a bright breakfast nook that's surrounded by views. French doors lead to an open porch and a sensational sunroom.

The nearby two-story great room includes a massive stone fireplace, floor-to-ceiling windows, and built-in bookshelves. French doors lead outside, extending the living space and inviting guests to enjoy the gentle breezes. Hardwood floors, recessed lighting, and 10-foot ceilings enhance the entire first floor.

Two staircases lead to the second floor, which offers a balcony overlook to the great room. Each of the two family bedrooms has a built-in bench or seat and plenty of wardrobe space. Compartmented lavatories provide each bedroom with private entrances to the shared bath. A gallery hall with built-in shelves leads to a guest suite with a large wardrobe and triple window. ∎

LEFT: The kitchen island overlooks the great room, allowing the family cook to remain involved in conversations during meal preparation. ABOVE: The simple yet elegant dining room, illuminated by an Arts & Crafts-style lamp, provides a built-in hutch.

DESIGN HPT9900002

STYLE: BUNGALOW
FIRST FLOOR: 2,597 SQ. FT.
SECOND FLOOR: 2,171 SQ. FT.
TOTAL: 4,768 SQ. FT.
BEDROOMS: 4
BATHROOMS: 4½
WIDTH: 76' - 6"
DEPTH: 68' - 6"
FOUNDATION: CRAWLSPACE

SEARCH ONLINE @ EPLANS.COM

FIRST FLOOR

SECOND FLOOR

LEFT: A stained-glass window with a simple pattern adds style to the front door. OPPOSITE PAGE: Exposed structural elements decorate the roofline of this bungalow.

ULTIMATE BUNGALOW

Reminiscent of the California bungalows designed by Greene & Greene, this modern plan honors Arts & Crafts style

Architects Charles & Henry Greene designed beautiful, practical bungalows that were rich in Craftsman detailing. This plan, though modern, would fit right in with their "ultimate bungalow" designs. The timber-framed porch and golden wood lend a charming rustic look to the exterior, which includes Craftsman-style decorative beams and porch pillars.

Inside, the expansive great room—in fine Arts & Crafts tradition—serves as the heart of the home. The room is arranged around a large hearth; other unique elements include gorgeous hardwood flooring, simple, sensible wood furnishings, and a soaring ceiling with exposed trusses. A magnificent window anchors one end of this room, providing the close relationship to nature that's so sought-after in Craftsman-style and bungalow plans. Hardwood flooring and exposed-beam ceilings, first seen in the great room, continue throughout the first-floor living spaces. To the right of the entry, the formal dining room creates

ABOVE: Hardwood flooring and simply crafted furnishings create harmony in the great room.
ABOVE RIGHT: Soft lights set in the coffered ceiling illuminate the dining room.

a welcoming atmosphere with soft lighting. Access to the outdoors is provided here as well, through doors that lead to the covered wraparound porch. The kitchen, brightened by a triple window over the sink, offers a central work island with built-in space for cookbook storage. Nearby, the nook, which opens to a rear deck, allows space for quiet meals. The great room, kitchen, and nook are all open to one another, creating one large multifunctional gathering area. To the left of the great room, a sunroom with access to a balcony provides even more space to enjoy the outdoors.

Sleeping quarters are just as comfortable and distinctive as the rest of the home; the master suite includes a volume ceiling, two walk-in closets, and a private bath with a compartmented toilet. The sunroom can be accessed through the master bath. A staircase off the foyer leads upstairs to two additional bedrooms, a full bath, and a lounge area. The third bedroom includes a walk-in closet and easy access to the bath. The lounge area allows dramatic views of the foyer and great room. ■

Built-in shelves and a counter that doubles as a breakfast bar maximizes space in the kitchen.

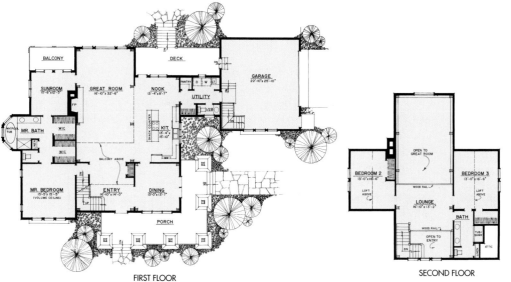

FIRST FLOOR

SECOND FLOOR

RECOMMENDED READING

The information presented in *Arts & Crafts Home Plans* serves as a general introduction to Craftsman, Bungalow, and Prairie-style architecture and interiors. For more in-depth coverage of the Arts & Crafts Movement, in England and in America, try the following books and Web sites.

American Bungalow magazine
www.ambungalow.com

The Craftsman Home
www.thecraftsmanhome.com
3048 Claremont Avenue
Berkeley, California 94705
1-510–655–6503

The Arts & Crafts Society
www.arts-crafts.com

Style 1900 magazine
www.style1900.com

A Field Guide to American Houses
By Virginia & Lee McAlester

50 Favorite Houses by Frank Lloyd Wright
By Diane Maddex

American Vernacular: Regional Influences in Architecture & Interior Design
By Jim Kemp

House Styles in America: The Old-House Journal Guide to the Architecture of American Homes
By James C. Massey and Shirley Maxwell

Living in the Arts & Crafts Style: A Home Decorating Workbook
By Charlotte Kelley

American Bungalow Style
By Robert Winter & Alexander Vertikoff

The New Bungalow
Essays by Matthew Bialecki, Christian Gladu, Jill Kessenich, Jim McCord, Su Bacon

The Arts & Crafts House
By Adrian Tinniswood

The Arts & Crafts Home
By Kitty Turgeon & Robert Rust

Classic Craftsman designs are all about simplicity, but this design combines a stunning Craftsman exterior with one of today's luxurious floor plans. The first floor has open spaces for living: a reading room and dining room flanking the foyer, a huge family room with built-ins and fireplace plus covered deck access, and an island kitchen and nook with built-in table. The first-floor master suite is graced with a beamed ceiling. Its attached bath is well appointed and spacious. On the second floor are four bedrooms and three baths. Third-floor attic space can be used for whatever suits you best. Don't miss the home theater that can be developed in the basement and home-office space over the garage.

DESIGN HPT9900003

STYLE: CRAFTSMAN
FIRST FLOOR: 2,120 SQ. FT.
SECOND FLOOR: 1,520 SQ. FT.
THIRD FLOOR: 183 SQ. FT.
TOTAL: 3,823 SQ. FT.
BEDROOMS: 5
BATHROOMS: 4½ + ½
WIDTH: 76' - 0"
DEPTH: 81' - 0"
FOUNDATION: BASEMENT, SLAB, CRAWLSPACE

SEARCH ONLINE @ EPLANS.COM

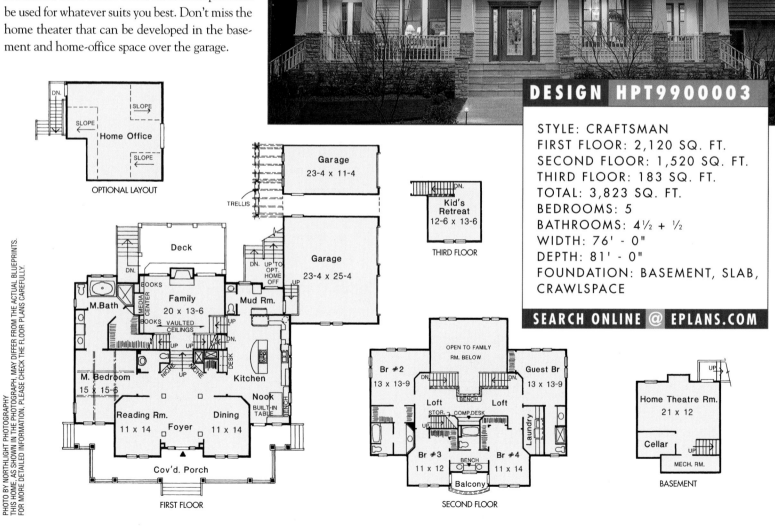

OPTIONAL LAYOUT

Home Office

Garage 23-4 x 11-4

TRELLIS

Garage 23-4 x 25-4

Kid's Retreat 12-6 x 13-6

THIRD FLOOR

Deck

M.Bath

Family 20 x 13-6 VAULTED CEILINGS

Mud Rm.

M. Bedroom 15 x 15-6

Kitchen

Nook BUILT-IN TABLE

Reading Rm. 11 x 14

Foyer

Dining 11 x 14

Cov'd. Porch

FIRST FLOOR

OPEN TO FAMILY RM. BELOW

Br #2 13 x 13-9

Guest Br 13 x 13-9

Loft

Loft

STOR. COMP.DESK

Laundry

Br #3 11 x 12

Br #4 11 x 14

BENCH

Balcony

SECOND FLOOR

Home Theatre Rm. 21 x 12

Cellar

MECH. RM.

BASEMENT

CRAFTSMAN

This charming Craftsman home would look great in any neighborhood! From the covered front porch, with a bench to rest on, to the trio of gables, this design has a lot of appeal. Inside, the Craftsman styling continues with built-in shelves in the study, a warming fireplace in the great room, and plenty of windows to bring in the outdoors. The L-shaped kitchen is open to the nook and great room, and offers easy access to the formal dining area. Upstairs, two family bedrooms share a full bath and access to both a laundry room and a large bonus room. A vaulted master suite rounds out this floor with class. Complete with a walk-in closet and a pampering bath, this suite will be a haven for any homeowner.

DESIGN HPT9900004

STYLE: CRAFTSMAN
FIRST FLOOR: 1,082 SQ. FT.
SECOND FLOOR: 864 SQ. FT.
TOTAL: 1,946 SQ. FT.
BONUS SPACE: 358 SQ. FT.
BEDROOMS: 3
BATHROOMS: 2½
WIDTH: 40' - 0"
DEPTH: 52' - 0"
FOUNDATION: CRAWLSPACE

SEARCH ONLINE @ EPLANS.COM

FIRST FLOOR

SECOND FLOOR

ORDER BLUEPRINTS 24 HOURS, 7 DAYS A WEEK, AT 1-800-521-6797

W ith rustic rafter tails, sturdy pillars, and a siding-and-shingle facade, this welcoming Craftsman plan offers plenty of curb appeal. Inside, the formal dining room sits to the left of the foyer and gives easy access to the angled kitchen. A spacious gathering room offers a fireplace, built-ins, a wall of windows, and access to a covered terrace. Located on the first floor for privacy, the master bedroom is lavish with its amenities, including His and Hers walk-in closets and basins, a garden tub, and a compartmented toilet. Upstairs, two suites offer private baths and share a linkside retreat that includes a fairway veranda.

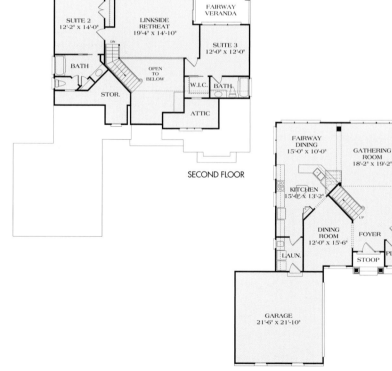

SECOND FLOOR

FIRST FLOOR

DESIGN HPT9900005

STYLE: CRAFTSMAN
FIRST FLOOR: 1,661 SQ. FT.
SECOND FLOOR: 882 SQ. FT.
TOTAL: 2,543 SQ. FT.
BEDROOMS: 3
BATHROOMS: 3½
WIDTH: 59' - 0"
DEPTH: 58' - 11"
FOUNDATION: CRAWLSPACE

SEARCH ONLINE @ EPLANS.COM

CRAFTSMAN

Horizontal siding, double-hung windows, and European gables lend a special charm to this Craftsman home. The formal dining room opens from the foyer and offers a wet bar and a box-bay window. The great room features a fireplace and opens to a golf porch as well as a charming side porch. A well-lit kitchen contains a cooktop island counter and two pantries. The first-floor master suite has a tray ceiling, a box-bay window, and a deluxe bath with a garden tub and an angled shower. Both of the upper-level bedrooms privately access a full bath.

DESIGN HPT9900087

STYLE: CRAFTSMAN
FIRST FLOOR: 1,824 SQ. FT.
SECOND FLOOR: 842 SQ. FT.
TOTAL: 2,666 SQ. FT.
BONUS SPACE: 267 SQ. FT.
BEDROOMS: 3
BATHROOMS: 3½
WIDTH: 59' - 0"
DEPTH: 53' - 6"
FOUNDATION: CRAWLSPACE

SEARCH ONLINE @ EPLANS.COM

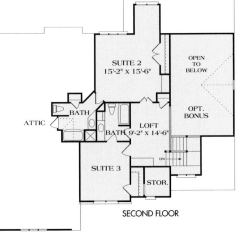

SECOND FLOOR

FIRST FLOOR

ORDER BLUEPRINTS 24 HOURS, 7 DAYS A WEEK, AT 1-800-521-6797

S hingles, stone, and gables, all elements of fine Craftsman styling, are beautifully demonstrated on this three-bedroom home. The foyer is flanked by a formal dining room and a cozy den. A galley kitchen is open to the spacious gathering room and sunny bayed nook. Upstairs, the secondary bedrooms share a hall bath. The master suite is full of amenities, including a sitting area with a private balcony, and a luxurious bath. A bonus room is located above the garage, perfect for a playroom, home office, or guest room.

DESIGN HPT9900007

STYLE: CRAFTSMAN
FIRST FLOOR: 1,170 SQ. FT.
SECOND FLOOR: 1,091 SQ. FT.
TOTAL: 2,261 SQ. FT.
BONUS SPACE: 240 SQ. FT.
BEDROOMS: 3
BATHROOMS: 2½
WIDTH: 66' - 0"
DEPTH: 46' - 0"
FOUNDATION: CRAWLSPACE

SEARCH ONLINE @ EPLANS.COM

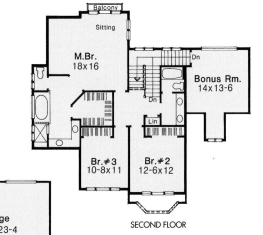

SECOND FLOOR

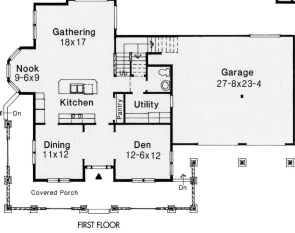

FIRST FLOOR

© Stephen Fuller, Inc.

This lovely Craftsman-style home invites enjoyment of the outdoors with a front covered porch and a spacious rear terrace. Inside, formal rooms flank the foyer and feature lovely amenities such as French-door access to the front porch. A fireplace warms the family room, which provides plenty of natural light and wide views through three sets of glass doors. The first-floor master suite features a large walk-in closet, sumptuous bath, and plenty of windows. Additional bedrooms on the second floor enjoy a balcony overlook to the family room.

DESIGN HPT9900008

STYLE: CRAFTSMAN
FIRST FLOOR: 1,924 SQ. FT.
SECOND FLOOR: 1,097 SQ. FT.
TOTAL: 3,021 SQ. FT.
BONUS SPACE: 352 SQ. FT.
BEDROOMS: 3
BATHROOMS: 2½
WIDTH: 68' - 3"
DEPTH: 53' - 0"
FOUNDATION: CRAWLSPACE

SEARCH ONLINE @ EPLANS.COM

Interesting rooflines, a porte cochere, front and rear covered porches, and an angled entry are just the beginning of this Craftsman design. The great room welcomes all with its fireplace and windowed views. The efficient kitchen includes access to the formal dining room, a breakfast nook, and a snack bar. An impressive master bedroom has French doors that open to a small entry area that could be used for a study, nursery, or sitting room. Two bedrooms on the upper level share a full bath and a study loft.

DESIGN HPT9900009

L D

STYLE: CRAFTSMAN
FIRST FLOOR: 1,836 SQ. FT.
SECOND FLOOR: 600 SQ. FT.
TOTAL: 2,436 SQ. FT.
BEDROOMS: 3
BATHROOMS: 2½
WIDTH: 86' - 7"
DEPTH: 54' - 0"
FOUNDATION: BASEMENT

SEARCH ONLINE @ EPLANS.COM

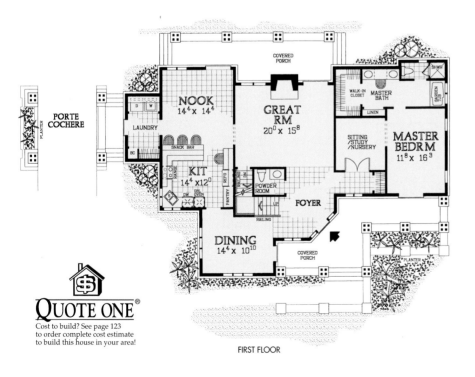

FIRST FLOOR

QUOTE ONE®
Cost to build? See page 123
to order complete cost estimate
to build this house in your area!

SECOND FLOOR

CRAFTSMAN

DESIGN HPT9900010

STYLE: CRAFTSMAN
FIRST FLOOR: 2,222 SQ. FT.
SECOND FLOOR: 1,235 SQ. FT.
TOTAL: 3,457 SQ. FT.
BEDROOMS: 4
BATHROOMS: 3½
WIDTH: 70' - 0"
DEPTH: 100' - 6"
FOUNDATION: CRAWLSPACE

SEARCH ONLINE @ EPLANS.COM

Sturdy pillars, stone accents, and gable detailing announce this design's Craftsman influences. Inside, the vaulted great room boasts a fireplace and built-in media center, and opens to the rear property through two sets of doors. Nearby, the breakfast nook—with access to a covered porch—adjoins a spacious island kitchen. The first-floor master suite provides a bay window, two walk-in closets, and a private bath with a compartmented toilet. Upstairs, a second master suite—also with a private bath—joins two additional bedrooms, one of which can double as a study.

SECOND FLOOR

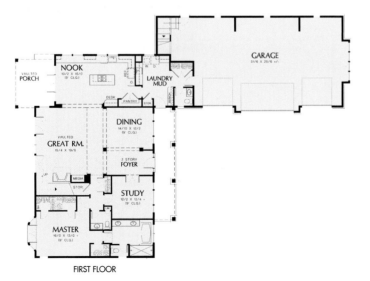

FIRST FLOOR

ORDER BLUEPRINTS 24 HOURS, 7 DAYS A WEEK, AT 1-800-521-6797

Craftsman-style windows and pillars, along with shingles and stone, enhance the exterior of this spacious plan. The open floor plan allows the formal dining room to flow gracefully through a columned area to the two-story great room, which includes a fireplace, built-in media center, and access to the outdoors. The kitchen offers a walk-in pantry, complete with a sink, and adjoins a breakfast nook. A split-bedroom plan on the first floor places the vaulted master suite and its private bath to the right and an additional bedroom with a walk-in closet to the left. Two second-floor bedrooms have easy access to a den with a wet bar.

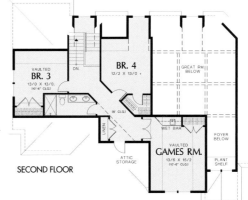

DESIGN HPT9900011

STYLE: CRAFTSMAN
FIRST FLOOR: 2,950 SQ. FT.
SECOND FLOOR: 943 SQ. FT.
TOTAL: 3,893 SQ. FT.
BEDROOMS: 4
BATHROOMS: 3½
WIDTH: 75' - 0"
DEPTH: 83' - 0"
FOUNDATION: CRAWLSPACE

SEARCH ONLINE @ EPLANS.COM

FIRST FLOOR

SECOND FLOOR

CRAFTSMAN

Perfect for a sloping lot, this Craftsman design boasts two levels of living space. Plenty of special amenities—vaulted ceilings in the living, dining, and family rooms, as well as in the master bedroom; built-ins in the family room and den; a large island cooktop in the kitchen; and an expansive rear deck—make this plan stand out. All three of the bedrooms—a main-level master suite and two lower-level bedrooms—include walk-in closets. Also on the lower level, find a recreation room with built-ins and a fireplace.

DESIGN HPT9900012

STYLE: CRAFTSMAN
MAIN LEVEL: 2,170 SQ. FT.
LOWER LEVEL: 1,076 SQ. FT.
TOTAL: 3,246 SQ. FT.
BEDROOMS: 3
BATHROOMS: 2½
WIDTH: 74' - 0"
DEPTH: 54' - 0"
FOUNDATION: SLAB, BASEMENT

SEARCH ONLINE @ EPLANS.COM

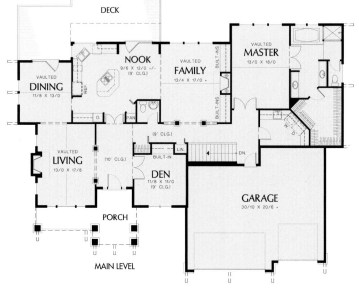

MAIN LEVEL

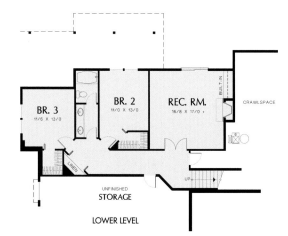

LOWER LEVEL

A covered front porch provides a welcoming entry for this Craftsman design, which features a stunning amenity-filled interior. Vaulted ceilings adorn the great room, office, and even the garage; the dining room includes a built-in hutch, and the kitchen boasts a walk-in pantry. Upstairs, the master suite offers a walk-in closet with built-in shelves, along with a private bath that contains a spa tub; two additional bedrooms also have walk-in closets. A fourth bedroom, a recreation room with a fireplace and wet bar, and a wine cellar reside on the lower level.

DESIGN HPT9900013

STYLE: CRAFTSMAN
MAIN LEVEL: 1,268 SQ. FT.
UPPER LEVEL: 931 SQ. FT.
LOWER LEVEL: 949 SQ. FT.
TOTAL: 3,148 SQ. FT.
BEDROOMS: 4
BATHROOMS: 3½
WIDTH: 53' - 6"
DEPTH: 73' - 0"
FOUNDATION: BASEMENT

SEARCH ONLINE @ EPLANS.COM

UPPER LEVEL

MAIN LEVEL

LOWER LEVEL

CRAFTSMAN

This striking Craftsman plan enjoys many charms that will make it a place you'll long to come home to. The country kitchen, for example, is a real delight. It enjoys a handy island counter, a serving bar to the family room, and two pantries—one a butler's pantry, making service to the formal dining room especially efficient. Plant shelves in the upstairs master bath could help make this a semitropical retreat. A downstairs study—or make it a guest bedroom—has hall access to a full bath. Two more second-floor bedrooms with walk-in closets share a bath.

DESIGN HPT9900014

STYLE: CRAFTSMAN
FIRST FLOOR: 1,404 SQ. FT.
SECOND FLOOR: 959 SQ. FT.
TOTAL: 2,363 SQ. FT.
BONUS SPACE: 374 SQ. FT.
BEDROOMS: 4
BATHROOMS: 3
WIDTH: 56' - 10"
DEPTH: 45' - 6"
FOUNDATION: CRAWLSPACE, BASEMENT

SEARCH ONLINE @ EPLANS.COM

SECOND FLOOR

FIRST FLOOR

Come home to this delightful plan, created with you in mind. From the covered front porch, the foyer opens to the dining room on the left and vaulted family room ahead. An elongated island in the well-planned kitchen makes meal preparation a joy. A sunny breakfast nook is perfect for casual pursuits. Tucked to the rear, the master suite enjoys ultimate privacy and a luxurious break from the world with a vaulted bath and garden tub. Secondary bedrooms share a full bath upstairs; a bonus room is ready to expand as your needs change.

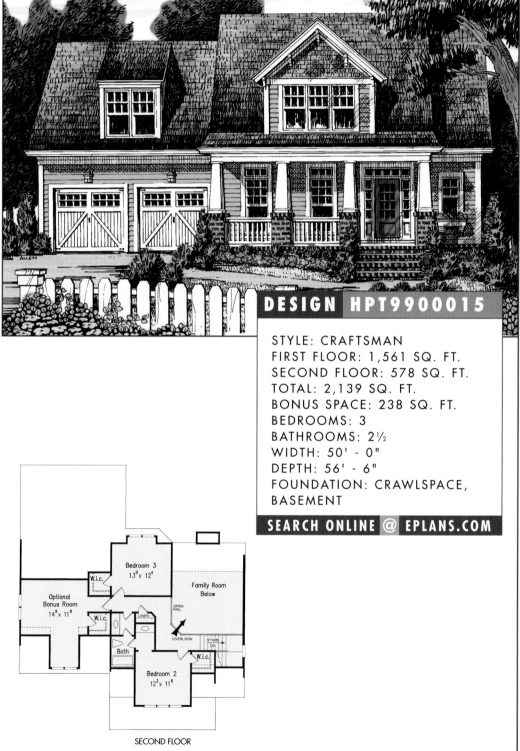

DESIGN HPT9900015

STYLE: CRAFTSMAN
FIRST FLOOR: 1,561 SQ. FT.
SECOND FLOOR: 578 SQ. FT.
TOTAL: 2,139 SQ. FT.
BONUS SPACE: 238 SQ. FT.
BEDROOMS: 3
BATHROOMS: 2½
WIDTH: 50' - 0"
DEPTH: 56' - 6"
FOUNDATION: CRAWLSPACE, BASEMENT

SEARCH ONLINE @ EPLANS.COM

FIRST FLOOR

SECOND FLOOR

CRAFTSMAN

Soaring ceilings help accent the spaciousness of this impressive two-story Craftsman design. Two fireplaces—one in the vaulted keeping room, the other flanked by radius transoms in the family room—create a cozy atmosphere. The centrally positioned kitchen enjoys an island counter, serving bar, loads of counter space, and, best of all, a walk-in pantry. The entire left wing embraces the resplendent master suite; upstairs, three more bedrooms, all with walk-in closets, offer ample sleeping space for children or guests. Two baths and space for future development are also located on this floor.

DESIGN HPT9900016

STYLE: CRAFTSMAN
FIRST FLOOR: 1,909 SQ. FT.
SECOND FLOOR: 835 SQ. FT.
TOTAL: 2,744 SQ. FT.
BEDROOMS: 4
BATHROOMS: 3½
WIDTH: 56' - 0"
DEPTH: 51' - 4"
FOUNDATION: CRAWLSPACE, BASEMENT

SEARCH ONLINE @ EPLANS.COM

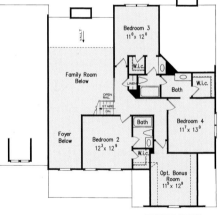

SECOND FLOOR

FIRST FLOOR

ORDER BLUEPRINTS 24 HOURS, 7 DAYS A WEEK, AT 1-800-521-6797

Craftsman-style pillars and windows lend a classic look to this home. An elegant entry opens to the vaulted family room, where a fireplace warms and bright windows illuminate. The kitchen is designed for the true chef, with step-saving orientation and a serving bar to the vaulted breakfast nook. A bedroom nearby is ideal for a home office or live-in help. The master suite is on the left, pampering with a vaulted bath and enormous walk-in closet. Two bedrooms upstairs share a full bath and an optional bonus room.

DESIGN HPT9900017

STYLE: CRAFTSMAN
FIRST FLOOR: 1,761 SQ. FT.
SECOND FLOOR: 577 SQ. FT.
TOTAL: 2,338 SQ. FT.
BONUS SPACE: 305 SQ. FT.
BEDROOMS: 4
BATHROOMS: 3
WIDTH: 56' - 0"
DEPTH: 48' - 0"
FOUNDATION: CRAWLSPACE, BASEMENT

SEARCH ONLINE @ EPLANS.COM

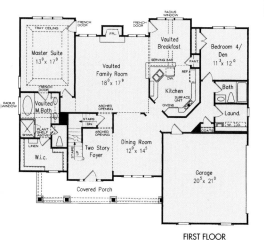

FIRST FLOOR

SECOND FLOOR

CRAFTSMAN

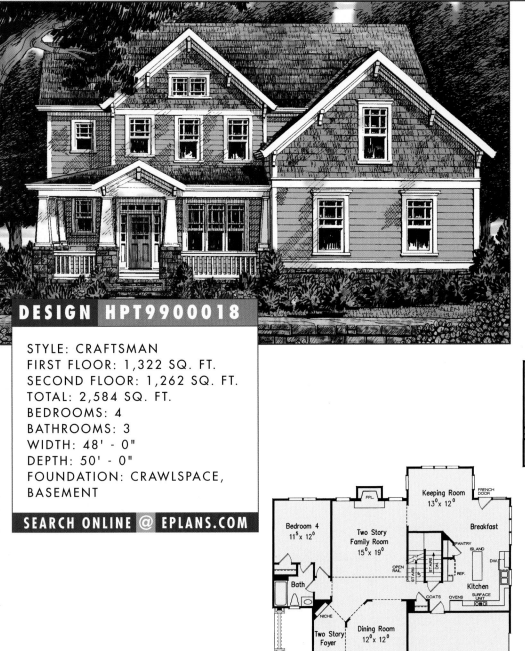

DESIGN HPT9900018

STYLE: CRAFTSMAN
FIRST FLOOR: 1,322 SQ. FT.
SECOND FLOOR: 1,262 SQ. FT.
TOTAL: 2,584 SQ. FT.
BEDROOMS: 4
BATHROOMS: 3
WIDTH: 48' - 0"
DEPTH: 50' - 0"
FOUNDATION: CRAWLSPACE,
BASEMENT

SEARCH ONLINE @ EPLANS.COM

With Craftsman detail and traditional charm, this four-bedroom home captures the comfort and style you've been searching for. From a wrapping porch, enter the two-story foyer with a decorative niche that displays special photos or treasures to all your guests. Continue to a beautiful family room, graced with a two-story ceiling and second-floor radius windows. The kitchen is open and spacious, leading to a breakfast area, hearth-warmed keeping room, and elegant dining room. A bedroom on this level also serves as an ideal den or home office. Upstairs, two secondary bedrooms share a full bath. The master suite is ready for relaxation with a sunny sitting room and soothing vaulted bath. A laundry room on this level makes wash day a breeze.

SECOND FLOOR

Sitting Room 13⁰ x 12⁰
Bedroom 3 11⁵ x 12¹⁰
Family Room Below
Master Suite 13⁵ x 17⁰
Bath
Foyer Below
Bedroom 2 12⁰ x 12⁰
Laund.
Vaulted M.Bath
W.i.c.

FIRST FLOOR

Keeping Room 13⁰ x 12⁰
Bedroom 4 11⁵ x 12⁰
Two Story Family Room 15⁰ x 19⁰
Breakfast
Kitchen
Bath
Two Story Foyer
Dining Room 12⁰ x 12⁰
Garage 20⁵ x 21⁹
Covered Porch

ORDER BLUEPRINTS 24 HOURS, 7 DAYS A WEEK, AT 1-800-521-6797

Brick pillars line the front porch of this vintage Craftsman home, and flower-box windows add undeniable country charm. Inside, the two-story foyer opens on either side to formal rooms, adorned with columns. A touch of elegance graces the family room, where a coffered ceiling and built-in-framed fireplace create a welcoming atmosphere. Opening to the breakfast bay is the island kitchen, enjoying a plentiful pantry. Three secondary bedrooms on the upper level provide space for family and guests, including a generous suite. The master suite soothes with a vaulted sitting area and bath, and a walk-in closet with more than ample storage. A laundry room is located on this level for extra convenience.

DESIGN HPT9900019

STYLE: CRAFTSMAN
FIRST FLOOR: 1,335 SQ. FT.
SECOND FLOOR: 1,572 SQ. FT.
TOTAL: 2,907 SQ. FT.
BEDROOMS: 4
BATHROOMS: 3½
WIDTH: 55' - 0"
DEPTH: 45' - 0"
FOUNDATION: CRAWLSPACE, BASEMENT

SEARCH ONLINE @ EPLANS.COM

FIRST FLOOR

SECOND FLOOR

CRAFTSMAN

DESIGN HPT9900020

STYLE: CRAFTSMAN
FIRST FLOOR: 1,243 SQ. FT.
SECOND FLOOR: 1,474 SQ. FT.
TOTAL: 2,717 SQ. FT.
BEDROOMS: 4
BATHROOMS: 3½
WIDTH: 46' - 4"
DEPTH: 66' - 0"
FOUNDATION: CRAWLSPACE,
BASEMENT

SEARCH ONLINE @ EPLANS.COM

There's an old-fashioned, settled-in feel about this two-story Craftsman home. The inviting front porch will bring hours of quiet relaxation. An impressive barrel vault ceiling highlights the hallway, which opens to a coat closet and half-bath and leads to both a stairway and the spacious family room. The breakfast alcove is marked off from the kitchen by an angled serving bar. Upstairs, the absolutely modern master suite enjoys separate sitting and sleeping areas, each with tray ceilings; French doors lead into the amenity-packed bath. Under a vaulted ceiling a garden bath, shower, and two vanities will bring soothing relaxation; a radius window artfully draws in natural light. Tucked in a rear corner of the first floor is a laundry that can be entered either from the breakfast/kitchen area or from outside through a small rear covered porch.

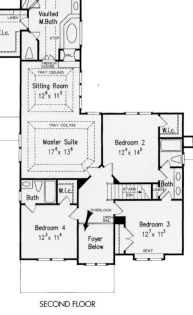

SECOND FLOOR

FIRST FLOOR

Stylish windows and rooflines on the exterior and elegant arches inside reflect the designer's goal of giving you a good-looking, comfortable home. From the two-story foyer, enter the formal living and dining rooms through wide arched entries. Straight ahead, another arched entry takes you into the family room. The family room, breakfast area, and kitchen are a trio running along the entire rear of the plan; a classy arch marks the line between the family room and the others. Upstairs, the bright and airy master suite enjoys a vaulted sitting area and private access to a covered porch. Three more bedrooms, a bath, and a convenient laundry are also situated on this floor. The two-car garage can be accessed from either the kitchen or the dining room.

DESIGN HPT9900021

STYLE: CRAFTSMAN
FIRST FLOOR: 1,249 SQ. FT.
SECOND FLOOR: 1,458 SQ. FT.
TOTAL: 2,707 SQ. FT.
BEDROOMS: 4
BATHROOMS: 2½
WIDTH: 57' - 4"
DEPTH: 39' - 0"
FOUNDATION: CRAWLSPACE,
BASEMENT

SEARCH ONLINE @ EPLANS.COM

FIRST FLOOR

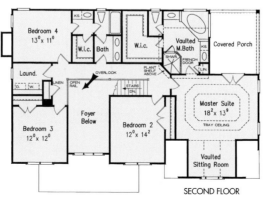

SECOND FLOOR

CRAFTSMAN

This Craftsman home is enhanced with unique pillars, horizontal siding, square clerestory windows, and muntin windows. Covered porches grace both the front and rear. Two doors access the spacious living room, where a fireplace heats up the space. The dining room and kitchen run into one smooth area and the kitchen accesses the rear covered porch. The right side of the plan is devoted to sleeping quarters: a master suite, with a private full bath, and two additional bedrooms, complete with walk-in closets.

DESIGN HPT9900022

STYLE: CRAFTSMAN
SQUARE FOOTAGE: 1,657
BEDROOMS: 3
BATHROOMS: 2
WIDTH: 64' - 0"
DEPTH: 58' - 0"
FOUNDATION: BASEMENT,
CRAWLSPACE, SLAB

SEARCH ONLINE @ EPLANS.COM

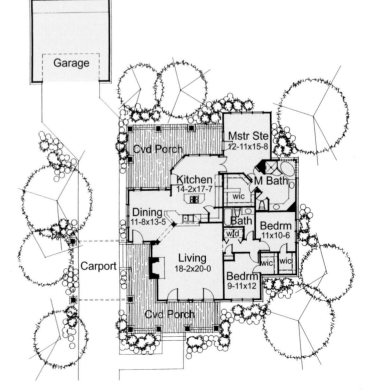

Shingles, window detail, gabled rooflines, and an attractively covered front porch all combine to give this home plenty of curb appeal. The floor plan inside is also an eye-catcher, with a U-shaped kitchen featuring a cooktop island and sharing a through-fireplace with the spacious great room. Here, a cathedral ceiling, a balcony from the second floor, and access to the rear porch all enhance an already welcoming ambiance. Formal and casual meals are easily taken care of in either the dining room, with a box-bay window, or the unique breakfast room. Located on the first floor for privacy, the master suite is full of amenities. Two large second-floor bedrooms—both with window seats—share a full bath complete with a dual-bowl vanity.

© 1997 Donald A. Gardner Architects, Inc.

DESIGN HPT9900023

STYLE: CRAFTSMAN
FIRST FLOOR: 1,608 SQ. FT.
SECOND FLOOR: 657 SQ. FT.
TOTAL: 2,265 SQ. FT.
BEDROOMS: 3
BATHROOMS: 2½
WIDTH: 56' - 4"
DEPTH: 70' - 5"

SEARCH ONLINE @ EPLANS.COM

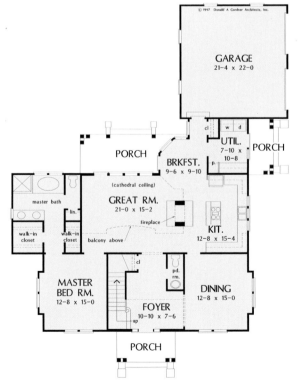

FIRST FLOOR

SECOND FLOOR

CRAFTSMAN

This alluring Craftsman home includes decorative stone detailing, noble pillars, and enchanting windows. The covered porch leads into the gallery, and just through the pillars is the great room, where the focal point is the fireplace. The kitchen features an island and a snack bar, with a breakfast nook nearby—a patio is accessible from the nook. A guest bedroom is located away from the family sleeping quarters for privacy. Two family bedrooms and a master suite reside on the left side of the plan.

DESIGN HPT9900024

STYLE: CRAFTSMAN
SQUARE FOOTAGE: 2,541
BEDROOMS: 4
BATHROOMS: 3
WIDTH: 81' - 0"
DEPTH: 54' - 0"
FOUNDATION: BASEMENT, SLAB, CRAWLSPACE

SEARCH ONLINE @ EPLANS.COM

You'll savor the timeless style of this charming Craftsman design. Inside, livability excels with a side-facing kitchen attached to a pleasant morning room. A formal dining room rests to the rear of the plan and enjoys direct access to a back porch. The parlor, with a central fireplace, also has access to this outdoor living area. The master bedroom offers a private bath with a walk-in closet, dual lavatories, and a bumped-out tub.

DESIGN HPT9900025

STYLE: CRAFTSMAN
SQUARE FOOTAGE: 2,135
BEDROOMS: 2
BATHROOMS: 2
WIDTH: 80' - 8"
DEPTH: 60' - 10"
FOUNDATION: BASEMENT

SEARCH ONLINE @ EPLANS.COM

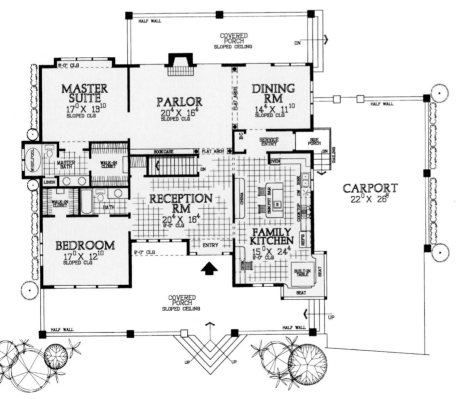

QUOTE ONE®
Cost to build? See page 123
to order complete cost estimate
to build this house in your area!

CRAFTSMAN

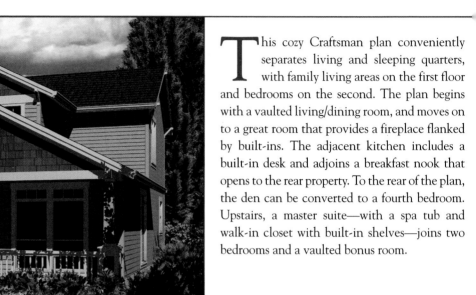

This cozy Craftsman plan conveniently separates living and sleeping quarters, with family living areas on the first floor and bedrooms on the second. The plan begins with a vaulted living/dining room, and moves on to a great room that provides a fireplace flanked by built-ins. The adjacent kitchen includes a built-in desk and adjoins a breakfast nook that opens to the rear property. To the rear of the plan, the den can be converted to a fourth bedroom. Upstairs, a master suite—with a spa tub and walk-in closet with built-in shelves—joins two bedrooms and a vaulted bonus room.

DESIGN HPT9900026

STYLE: CRAFTSMAN
FIRST FLOOR: 1,252 SQ. FT.
SECOND FLOOR: 985 SQ. FT.
TOTAL: 2,237 SQ. FT.
BONUS SPACE: 183 SQ. FT.
BEDROOMS: 4
BATHROOMS: 3
WIDTH: 40' - 0"
DEPTH: 51' - 0"
FOUNDATION: CRAWLSPACE, BASEMENT

SEARCH ONLINE @ EPLANS.COM

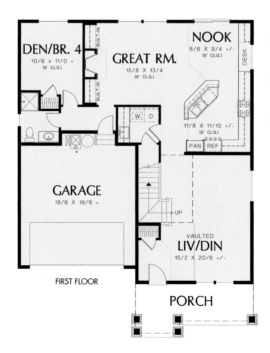

FIRST FLOOR

SECOND FLOOR

The decorative pillars and the wraparound porch are just the beginning of this comfortable Craftsman home. Inside, an angled U-shaped stairway leads to the second-floor sleeping zone. On the first floor, French doors lead to a bay-windowed den that shares a see-through fireplace with the two-story family room. The large island kitchen includes a writing desk, a corner sink, a breakfast nook, and access to the laundry room, the powder room, and the two-car garage. Upstairs, the master suite is a real treat with its French-door access, vaulted ceiling, and luxurious bath. Two other bedrooms and a full bath complete the second floor.

DESIGN HPT9900027

STYLE: CRAFTSMAN
FIRST FLOOR: 1,371 SQ. FT.
SECOND FLOOR: 916 SQ. FT.
TOTAL: 2,287 SQ. FT.
BEDROOMS: 3
BATHROOMS: 2½
WIDTH: 43' - 0"
DEPTH: 69' - 0"
FOUNDATION: CRAWLSPACE

SEARCH ONLINE @ EPLANS.COM

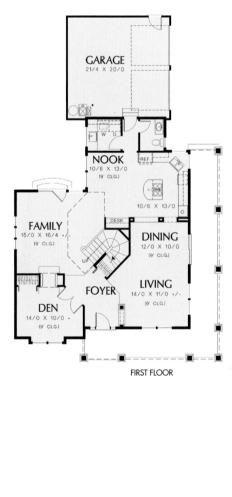

FIRST FLOOR

SECOND FLOOR

QUOTE ONE®
Cost to build? See page 123
to order complete cost estimate
to build this house in your area!

CRAFTSMAN

This compact Craftsman beauty offers ample space and comfort for family living. Three bedrooms—two upstairs and a master suite with a walk-in closet and private bath on the main level—are designed for convenience and charm. An open layout for the kitchen, eating nook, and family room give lots of flexibility for placement of furniture and other furnishings. A formal dining room and cozy den are situated in front just off the foyer. The plan comes with an option for a gas-vent fireplace in the family room.

DESIGN HPT9900028

STYLE: CRAFTSMAN
SQUARE FOOTAGE: 1,759
BEDROOMS: 3
BATHROOMS: 2½
WIDTH: 56' - 0"
DEPTH: 46' - 0"
FOUNDATION:
CRAWLSPACE, SLAB

SEARCH ONLINE @ EPLANS.COM

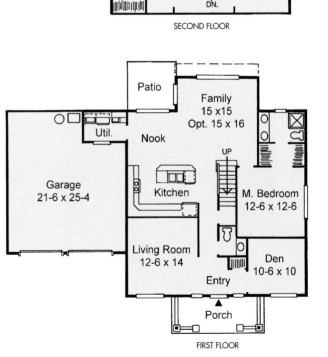

SECOND FLOOR

Br. #3
11-4 x 12

Br. #2
10-2 x 12-6

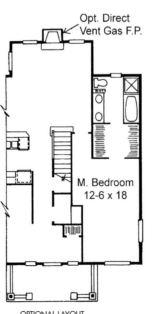

Opt. Direct
Vent Gas F.P.

M. Bedroom
12-6 x 18

OPTIONAL LAYOUT

Patio

Family
15 x15
Opt. 15 x 16

Util.

Nook

Garage
21-6 x 25-4

Kitchen

UP

M. Bedroom
12-6 x 12-6

Living Room
12-6 x 14

Den
10-6 x 10

Entry

Porch

FIRST FLOOR

A covered porch introduces this two-story Craftsman home and complements the horizontal wood siding with vertical siding trim. Inside, an open floor plan reigns. The vaulted living room is to the front where double doors open to the porch. Columns separate the living room from the formal dining room and the family room from the main hall. A corner fireplace and built-in shelves adorn the family room. The nook has sliding glass doors to the rear yard and is open to the kitchen. Three family bedrooms, a master suite, and a den are on the second floor. Note the walk-in closet and sumptuous bath in the master suite.

DESIGN HPT9900029

STYLE: CRAFTSMAN
FIRST FLOOR: 1,072 SQ. FT.
SECOND FLOOR: 1,108 SQ. FT.
TOTAL: 2,180 SQ. FT.
BEDROOMS: 4
BATHROOMS: 2½
WIDTH: 40' - 0"
DEPTH: 48' - 6"
FOUNDATION: CRAWLSPACE

SEARCH ONLINE @ EPLANS.COM

FIRST FLOOR

SECOND FLOOR

CRAFTSMAN

Two gables, supported by pillars and accented with rafter tails, are fine examples of Craftsmanship presented on this three-bedroom home. Inside, a den opens to the left of the foyer, providing a quiet place for relaxing. A living room with a fireplace flanked by windows welcomes casual times. The unique kitchen offers a small, yet cozy nook as well as ease in serving the dining room. The master suite is also on this floor and features a walk-in closet and a pampering bath. Downstairs, a huge recreation room is available for fun and stylish entertainment.

DESIGN HPT9900030

STYLE: CRAFTSMAN
MAIN LEVEL: 1,416 SQ. FT.
LOWER LEVEL: 1,300 SQ. FT.
TOTAL: 2,716 SQ. FT.
BEDROOMS: 3
BATHROOMS: 2½
WIDTH: 50' - 0"
DEPTH: 46' - 0"
FOUNDATION: BASEMENT

SEARCH ONLINE @ EPLANS.COM

3 Car Garage
33'-4" x 20'-8"

OPTIONAL LAYOUT

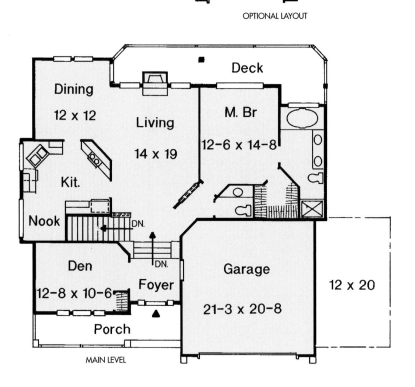

Deck

Dining
12 x 12

Living
14 x 19

M. Br
12-6 x 14-8

Kit.

Nook

DN.

DN.

Den
12-8 x 10-6

Foyer

Garage
21-3 x 20-8

12 x 20

Porch

MAIN LEVEL

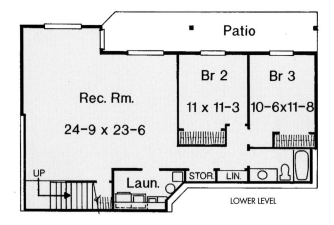

Patio

Rec. Rm.
24-9 x 23-6

Br 2
11 x 11-3

Br 3
10-6x11-8

UP

Laun.

STOR.

LIN.

LOWER LEVEL

This down-home, one-story Craftsman plan has all the comforts and necessities for solid family living. The vaulted family room, along with the adjoining country-style kitchen and breakfast nook, is at the center of the plan. The extended hearth fireplace flanked by radius windows will make this a cozy focus for family get-togethers and entertaining visitors. A formal dining room is marked off by decorative columns. The resplendent master suite assumes the entire right wing, where it is separated from two bedrooms located on the other side of the home. Built-in plant shelves in the master bath create a garden-like environment. Additional space is available for building another bedroom or study.

DESIGN HPT9900031

STYLE: CRAFTSMAN
SQUARE FOOTAGE: 1,724
BONUS SPACE: 375 SQ. FT.
BEDROOMS: 3
BATHROOMS: 2
WIDTH: 53' - 6"
DEPTH: 58' - 6"
FOUNDATION: CRAWLSPACE, BASEMENT

SEARCH ONLINE @ EPLANS.COM

CRAFTSMAN

Craftsman details such as stone supports and trim and woodwork in the gables lend a hearty welcome to guests and homeowners. A bench swing would suit the covered front porch. The entry provides privacy to the interior, separating the master suite from the remainder of the home via a short hallway. The hearth-warmed family room enjoys a built-in entertainment center and a lovely view of the backyard. The breakfast room accesses the rear covered porch. Nearby, the L-shaped kitchen features an island. Two family bedrooms to the front of the home share a full hall bath.

DESIGN HPT9900032

STYLE: CRAFTSMAN
SQUARE FOOTAGE: 1,724
BEDROOMS: 3
BATHROOMS: 2
WIDTH: 50' - 0"
DEPTH: 50' - 0"

SEARCH ONLINE @ EPLANS.COM

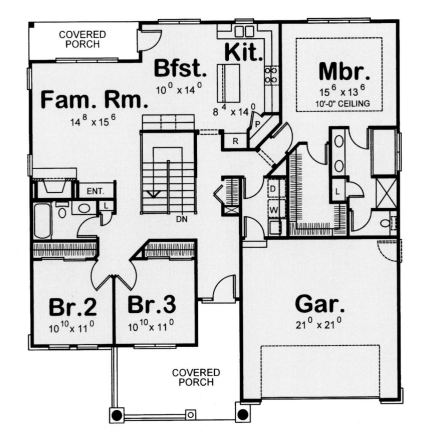

This two-story home offers a livable floor plan for both family gatherings and privacy. On the first floor a den is nestled behind French doors, and around the corner the great room provides a fireplace and an open area to the breakfast room. The U-shaped kitchen boasts a window sink and a snack bar. The master bedroom contains a private bath with dual vanities and a walk-in closet. Upstairs are three family bedrooms, a game room, and two full baths.

DESIGN HPT9900033

STYLE: CRAFTSMAN
FIRST FLOOR: 1,538 SQ. FT.
SECOND FLOOR: 748 SQ. FT.
TOTAL: 2,286 SQ. FT.
BONUS SPACE: 242 SQ. FT.
BEDROOMS: 4
BATHROOMS: 3½
WIDTH: 48' - 4"
DEPTH: 50' - 0"

SEARCH ONLINE @ EPLANS.COM

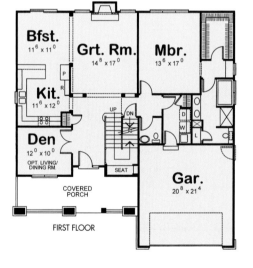

FIRST FLOOR

SECOND FLOOR

CRAFTSMAN

Elements of the Shingle style reside in this lovely Craftsman home, which captures a sense of casual dignity. The foyer opens to the formal rooms and to a secluded den or guest room. A vaulted family room adjoins a galley-style kitchen and a morning nook that accesses the outdoors. Sleeping quarters are connected by a hall leading back to the foyer. The master bedroom enjoys a private bath—with garden tub, separate shower, dual basins, and compartmented toilet— and a walk-in closet. The laundry room provides convenient access to the three-car garage.

DESIGN HPT9900034

STYLE: CRAFTSMAN
SQUARE FOOTAGE: 1,997
BEDROOMS: 4
BATHROOMS: 2½
WIDTH: 60' - 0"
DEPTH: 51' - 0"
FOUNDATION: CRAWLSPACE, BASEMENT

SEARCH ONLINE @ EPLANS.COM

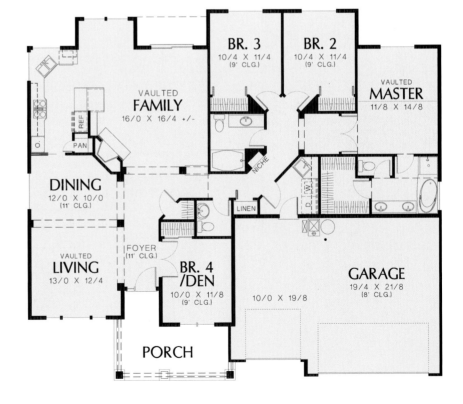

M odern amenities and an elegant floor plan define the interior of this design, which offers a classic Craftsman exterior. The vaulted great room, with a fireplace and built-in media center, shares a snack bar with the gourmet kitchen. The nearby breakfast nook includes sliding glass doors. The dining room also boasts a vaulted ceiling; add an optional wall and French doors to convert this room to a cozy den. The master suite, secluded to the right, contains a walk-in closet with built-in shelves, along with a private bath. Two secondary bedrooms, to the left of the plan, share a full bath and linen closet.

DESIGN HPT9900035

STYLE: CRAFTSMAN
SQUARE FOOTAGE: 1,771
BEDROOMS: 3
BATHROOMS: 2
WIDTH: 50' - 0"
DEPTH: 70' - 0"
FOUNDATION: CRAWLSPACE

SEARCH ONLINE @ EPLANS.COM

OPTIONAL LAYOUT

CRAFTSMAN

A contemporary plan with plenty of Craftsman elements, this home is especially suited for a growing family looking for comfort and convenience. For socializing, use the parlor, which enjoys a bay window overlooking the front porch. The family room, kitchen, and breakfast nook fit well together. Also located on the main level, the master suite offers a walk-in closet, dual-sink vanity, and separate shower and tub. Two bedrooms and a den—or make it another bedroom—share the upstairs with a bath and a recreation room with built-in desks, great for student-age youngsters.

DESIGN HPT9900036

STYLE: CRAFTSMAN
FIRST FLOOR: 1,280 SQ. FT.
SECOND FLOOR: 802 SQ. FT.
TOTAL: 2,082 SQ. FT.
BONUS SPACE: 228 SQ. FT.
BEDROOMS: 4
BATHROOMS: 2½
WIDTH: 40' - 0"
DEPTH: 49' - 0"
FOUNDATION: CRAWLSPACE

SEARCH ONLINE @ EPLANS.COM

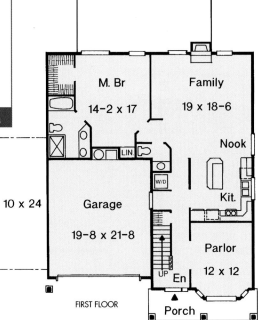

FIRST FLOOR

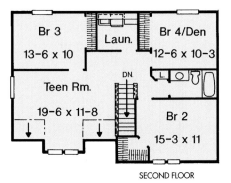

SECOND FLOOR

There's a lot of good living packed into this two-story Craftsman home. Arriving guests can be immediately ushered into the dining room (or make it a parlor) just off the grand foyer. At one end, the main living room is warmed by an extended-hearth fireplace; at the other, it flows into the dining area and is marked off from the kitchen by an angled island counter. It opens through French doors to the rear patio. The master suite, upstairs, enjoys a walk-in closet, lavish bath, and a spacious sitting room. Two other bedrooms share a bath. Located on the same level is a convenient laundry room and a possible study or recreation room for the home's youngsters.

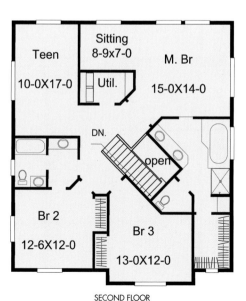

DESIGN HPT9900037

STYLE: CRAFTSMAN
FIRST FLOOR: 1,008 SQ. FT.
SECOND FLOOR: 1,129 SQ. FT.
TOTAL: 2,137 SQ. FT.
BONUS SPACE: 170 SQ. FT.
BEDROOMS: 3
BATHROOMS: 2½
WIDTH: 35' - 0"
DEPTH: 44' - 0"
FOUNDATION: CRAWLSPACE

SEARCH ONLINE @ EPLANS.COM

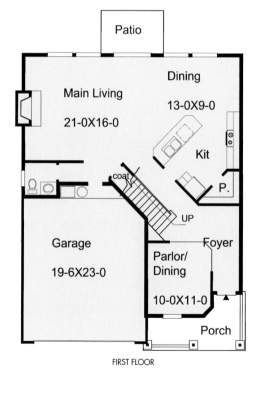

FIRST FLOOR

SECOND FLOOR

CRAFTSMAN

A charming dormer window accents the facade of this cozy Craftsman home. To the left of the foyer, double doors open to a den; choose built-in shelves or a convenient wall closet for this room. The central great room boasts a vaulted ceiling, built-in media center, and fireplace, and is open to the dining room, which features sliding glass dors that open to a side porch. A built-in desk adds convenience to the kitchen. Bedrooms to the left of the plan include a master suite, with a private bath and walk-in closet, and one additional bedroom.

DESIGN HPT9900038

STYLE: CRAFTSMAN
SQUARE FOOTAGE: 1,728
BEDROOMS: 2
BATHROOMS: 2
WIDTH: 55' - 0"
DEPTH: 48' - 0"
FOUNDATION: CRAWLSPACE

SEARCH ONLINE @ EPLANS.COM

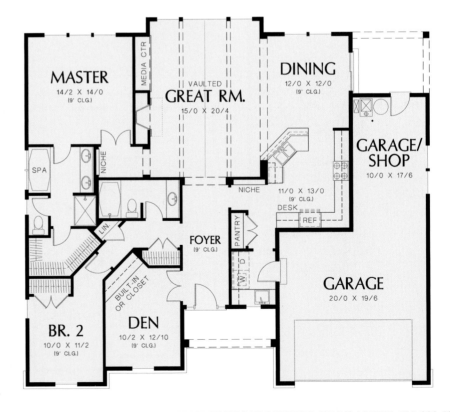

Craftsman-style windows with a bit of Palladian flair enhance the exterior of this home. Inside, a vaulted ceiling accents the formal living room; the adjoining dining room includes columns and a built-in display cabinet. The family room and nook, also with vaulted ceilings, serve as charming informal gathering areas. Sleeping quarters, to the left of the plan, include the vaulted master suite and two additional bedrooms. All three bedrooms are conveniently close to the utility room, which offers a wash sink and counter space.

DESIGN HPT9900039

STYLE: CRAFTSMAN
SQUARE FOOTAGE: 2,218
BEDROOMS: 3
BATHROOMS: 2
WIDTH: 50' - 0"
DEPTH: 70' - 0"
FOUNDATION: CRAWLSPACE

SEARCH ONLINE @ EPLANS.COM

CRAFTSMAN

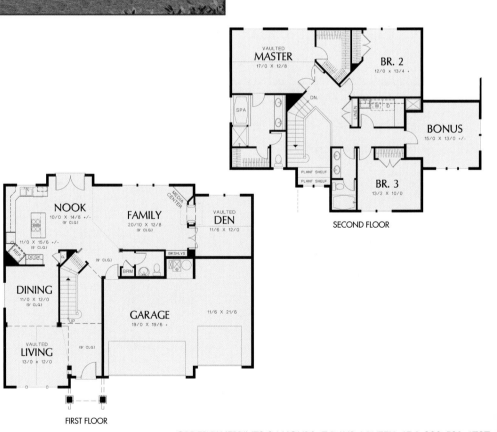

Three bedrooms, spacious family living areas, and plenty of amenities make this Craftsman design a pleasure to come home to. Vaulted ceilings enhance the den and living room, and built-in bookshelves, a media center, and a fireplace highlight the family room. The kitchen, with a built-in desk and island cooktop, serves the breakfast nook and dining room with ease. Sleeping quarters—the vaulted master suite and two family bedrooms—are upstairs, along with a bonus room and the utility area.

DESIGN HPT9900040

STYLE: CRAFTSMAN
FIRST FLOOR: 1,360 SQ. FT.
SECOND FLOOR: 1,154 SQ. FT.
TOTAL: 2,514 SQ. FT.
BONUS SPACE: 202 SQ. FT.
BEDROOMS: 3
BATHROOMS: 2½
WIDTH: 52' - 0"
DEPTH: 45' - 6"
FOUNDATION: CRAWLSPACE

SEARCH ONLINE @ EPLANS.COM

SECOND FLOOR

FIRST FLOOR

A sensible floor plan, with living spaces on the first floor and bedrooms on the second floor, is the highlight of this Craftsman home. Elegance reigns in the formal living room, with a vaulted ceiling and columned entry; this room is open to the dining room, which is brightened by natural light from two tall windows. Ideal for informal gatherings, the family room boasts a fireplace flanked by built-in shelves. The efficient kitchen includes a central island and double sink, and the nearby nook features easy access to the outdoors through sliding glass doors. The master suite includes a lavish bath with a corner spa tub and compartmented toilet; two additional bedrooms, one with a walk-in closet, share a full bath.

DESIGN HPT9900041

STYLE: CRAFTSMAN
FIRST FLOOR: 970 SQ. FT.
SECOND FLOOR: 988 SQ. FT.
TOTAL: 1,958 SQ. FT.
BEDROOMS: 3
BATHROOMS: 2½
WIDTH: 40' - 0"
DEPTH: 43' - 0"
FOUNDATION: CRAWLSPACE

SEARCH ONLINE @ EPLANS.COM

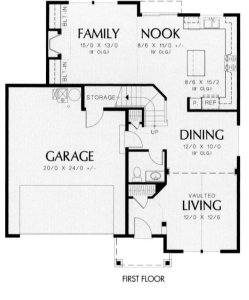

FIRST FLOOR

SECOND FLOOR

CRAFTSMAN

This charming Craftsman design offers a second-story master bedroom with four windows under the gabled dormer. The covered front porch displays column and pier supports. The hearth-warmed gathering room opens to the dining room on the right, where the adjoining kitchen offers enough space for an optional breakfast booth. A home office/guest suite is found in the rear. The second floor holds the lavish master suite and a second bedroom suite with its own private bath.

DESIGN HPT9900042

STYLE: CRAFTSMAN
FIRST FLOOR: 1,060 SQ. FT.
SECOND FLOOR: 914 SQ. FT.
TOTAL: 1,974 SQ. FT.
BEDROOMS: 3
BATHROOMS: 3
WIDTH: 32' - 0"
DEPTH: 35' - 0"
FOUNDATION: CRAWLSPACE

SEARCH ONLINE @ EPLANS.COM

GARAGE
20'-0" x 22'-0"

HOME OFFICE /
GUEST SUITE
13'-2" x 13'-10"

W.I.C.

PANT.

COVERED
PORCH

KITCHEN
12'-0" x 15'-8"

OPT. BUILT-IN
BREAKFAST
BOOTH

BATH

OPT.
2ND SINK

UP

OPT.
CABINETS

GATHERING
ROOM
18'-6" x 14'-4"

DINING
ROOM
12'-0" x 14'-4"

COVERED PORCH

FIRST FLOOR

MASTER
BATH

LIN

DN

SUITE 2
12'-2" x 13'-4"

W.I.C.

LAUN.

BATH

ATTIC
STOR.

MASTER
SUITE
14'-0" x 15'-8"

W.I.C.

ATTIC
STOR.

SECOND FLOOR

D on't be fooled by the small-looking exterior—this plan offers three bedrooms and plenty of living space. Notice that the screened porch leads to a rear terrace with access to the breakfast room. A living room/dining room combination adds spaciousness to the floor plan. Other welcome amenities include boxed windows in the breakfast room and dining room, a fireplace in the living room, a planning desk and pass-through snack bar in the kitchen, a whirlpool tub in the master bath, and an open two-story foyer. The thoughtfully placed flower box, beyond the kitchen window above the sink, adds a homespun touch to this already comfortable design.

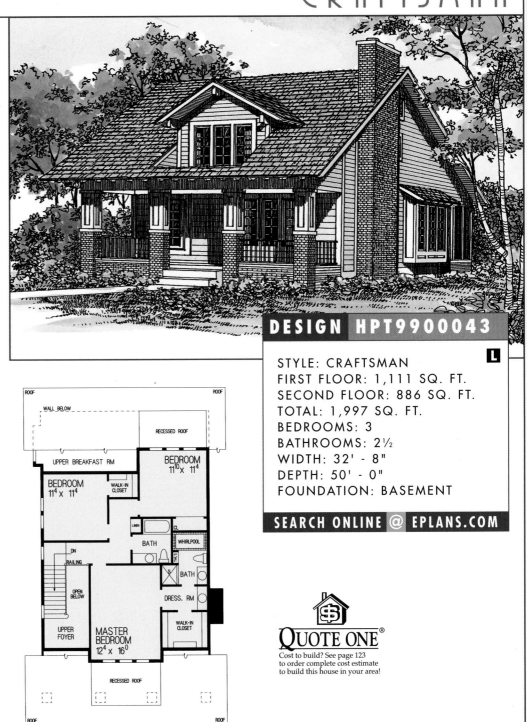

DESIGN HPT9900043

L

STYLE: CRAFTSMAN
FIRST FLOOR: 1,111 SQ. FT.
SECOND FLOOR: 886 SQ. FT.
TOTAL: 1,997 SQ. FT.
BEDROOMS: 3
BATHROOMS: 2½
WIDTH: 32' - 8"
DEPTH: 50' - 0"
FOUNDATION: BASEMENT

SEARCH ONLINE @ EPLANS.COM

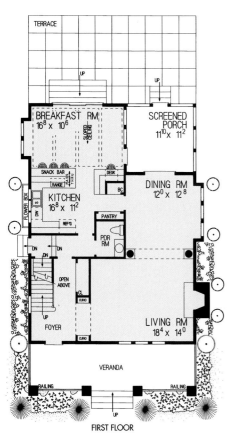

FIRST FLOOR

SECOND FLOOR

QUOTE ONE®
Cost to build? See page 123
to order complete cost estimate
to build this house in your area!

CRAFTSMAN

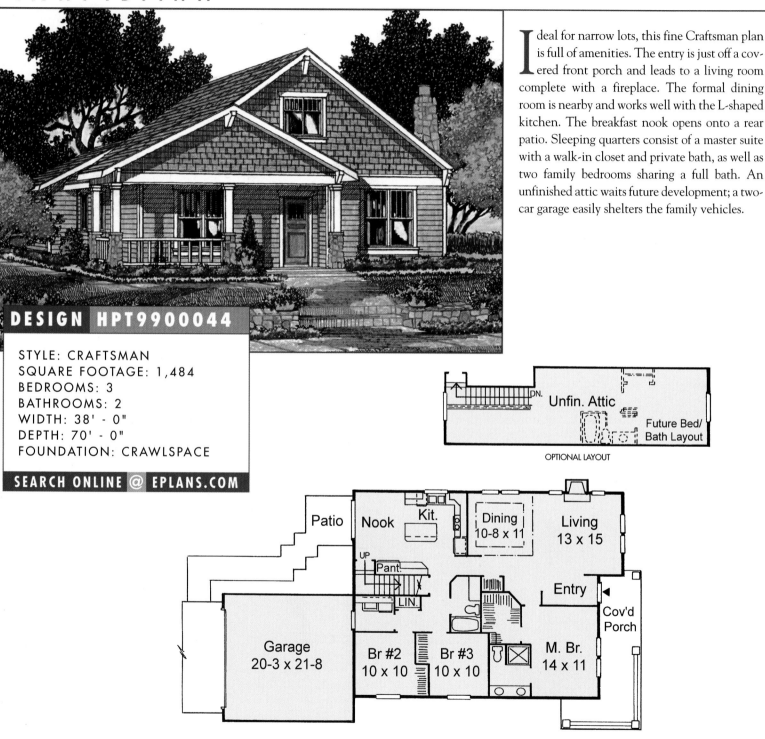

Ideal for narrow lots, this fine Craftsman plan is full of amenities. The entry is just off a covered front porch and leads to a living room complete with a fireplace. The formal dining room is nearby and works well with the L-shaped kitchen. The breakfast nook opens onto a rear patio. Sleeping quarters consist of a master suite with a walk-in closet and private bath, as well as two family bedrooms sharing a full bath. An unfinished attic waits future development; a two-car garage easily shelters the family vehicles.

DESIGN HPT9900044

STYLE: CRAFTSMAN
SQUARE FOOTAGE: 1,484
BEDROOMS: 3
BATHROOMS: 2
WIDTH: 38' - 0"
DEPTH: 70' - 0"
FOUNDATION: CRAWLSPACE

SEARCH ONLINE @ EPLANS.COM

Unfin. Attic

Future Bed/ Bath Layout

OPTIONAL LAYOUT

Patio

Nook

Kit.

Dining
10-8 x 11

Living
13 x 15

UP

Pant

LIN.

Entry

Cov'd Porch

Garage
20-3 x 21-8

Br #2
10 x 10

Br #3
10 x 10

M. Br.
14 x 11

This charming plan will not only fit onto a narrow lot, it also features many amenities. With shingles, rafter tails, and pillars supporting a covered front porch, its Craftsman influence is clearly evident. Inside, the foyer opens directly into the living room, where a fireplace adds cheer to any gathering. The formal dining room offers fine ceiling details and easy access to the efficient kitchen. Two family bedrooms share a hall bath, and the master suite comes with a walk-in closet and private bath. The attic has plenty of room for future expansion when it's needed. The two-car garage will easily shelter the family's vehicles.

DESIGN HPT9900045

STYLE: CRAFTSMAN
SQUARE FOOTAGE: 1,506
BEDROOMS: 3
BATHROOMS: 2
WIDTH: 44' - 0"
DEPTH: 53' - 0"
FOUNDATION: CRAWLSPACE

SEARCH ONLINE @ EPLANS.COM

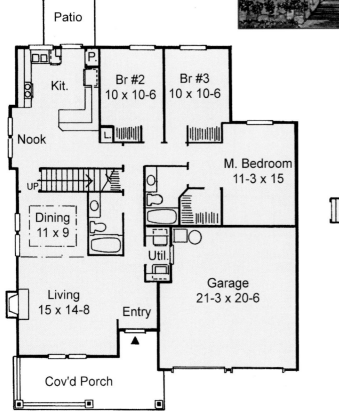

OPTIONAL LAYOUT

CRAFTSMAN

This handsome home is designed for easy living with a floor plan that puts the owner's comfort first. A quaint living and dining room is separated with a half-wall of built-in shelves. The large kitchen provides an open wet bar to the dining room and a snack bar to the combination breakfast/family room. The extra-large family room has sliding glass doors off the breakfast area and a door opening to the covered rear porch. The master bedroom offers privacy and convenience thanks to thoughtful first-floor planning. The two spacious bedrooms upstairs share a twin-basin bath.

Quote One®
Cost to build? See page 123 to order complete cost estimate to build this house in your area!

SECOND FLOOR

BEDRM 15⁴ x 11⁸

BEDRM 11⁶ x 11⁰

COVERED PORCH

MASTER BEDRM 13⁴ x 18⁰

FAMILY ROOM 15⁴ x 11⁶

BREAKFAST ROOM 15⁴ x 11⁸

MASTER BATH

KIT 13⁰ x 11⁴

WET BAR

DINING RM 13⁴ x 11⁰

5' HIGH SHELVES

LIVING RM 13⁴ x 11⁴

OPEN ABOVE

PDR

FOYER

COVERED PORCH

FIRST FLOOR

Get more out of your home-building dollars with this unique one-story plan. A covered front porch provides sheltered entry into the living room. The dining room enjoys a sloped ceiling, a wet bar, and direct access to the rear covered patio. The large master bedroom pampers with a sitting area, patio access, and a luxurious bath that features a corner tub, a separate shower, and dual lavatories. Two secondary bedrooms share a full hall bath.

DESIGN HPT9900047

L

STYLE: CRAFTSMAN
SQUARE FOOTAGE: 2,033
BEDROOMS: 3
BATHROOMS: 2
WIDTH: 47' - 6"
DEPTH: 61' - 6"
FOUNDATION: BASEMENT

SEARCH ONLINE @ EPLANS.COM

QUOTE ONE®
Cost to build? See page 123
to order complete cost estimate
to build this house in your area!

CRAFTSMAN

With its shingle siding and decorative front porch, this Craftsman delight will shine in any neighborhood. The spacious dining room is accessed by the well-equipped kitchen via the butler's pantry. In the rear, the more private and casual breakfast nook and gathering room create an open space for intimate entertaining. The master suite on the right offers a luxurious bath, twin walk-in closets, and a bumped-out window. Two secondary bedrooms share a full bath on the second floor.

DESIGN HPT9900048

STYLE: CRAFTSMAN
FIRST FLOOR: 1,478 SQ. FT.
SECOND FLOOR: 629 SQ. FT.
TOTAL: 2,107 SQ. FT.
BEDROOMS: 3
BATHROOMS: 2½
WIDTH: 32' - 0"
DEPTH: 59' - 0"
FOUNDATION: CRAWLSPACE

SEARCH ONLINE @ EPLANS.COM

SECOND FLOOR

FIRST FLOOR

The hipped roof of this two-story Craftsman home is accented with decorative knee-brace supports. The covered L-shaped porch, with its pier and column supports, shelters the entry from the elements. Inside, the gathering room and dining room are open, lending a casual air. The galley kitchen is flanked by the sunny breakfast nook and the dining room. The master suite has direct access to the front porch. Bedroom suites 2 and 3 share a Jack-and-Jill bath on the second floor.

DESIGN HPT9900049

STYLE: CRAFTSMAN
FIRST FLOOR: 1,283 SQ. FT.
SECOND FLOOR: 541 SQ. FT.
TOTAL: 1,824 SQ. FT.
BEDROOMS: 3
BATHROOMS: 2½
WIDTH: 32' - 0"
DEPTH: 49' - 8"
FOUNDATION: CRAWLSPACE

SEARCH ONLINE @ EPLANS.COM

BUNGALOW

W ith woodsy charm and cozy livability, this bungalow plan offers comfortable living space in a smaller footprint. The exterior is geared for outdoor fun, with two flagstone patios connected by a two-way fireplace and graced by a built-in barbecue. French doors on two sides lead into the large playroom, which features a kitchen area, washer and dryer space, and a bath with corner sink and shower. Take the L-shaped stairway to the bunk room upstairs, where there is space for sleeping and relaxing.

DESIGN HPT9900050

STYLE: BUNGALOW
FIRST FLOOR: 665 SQ. FT.
SECOND FLOOR: 395 SQ. FT.
TOTAL: 1,060 SQ. FT.
BEDROOMS: 1
BATHROOMS: 1
WIDTH: 34' - 3"
DEPTH: 32' - 5"
FOUNDATION: SLAB

SEARCH ONLINE @ EPLANS.COM

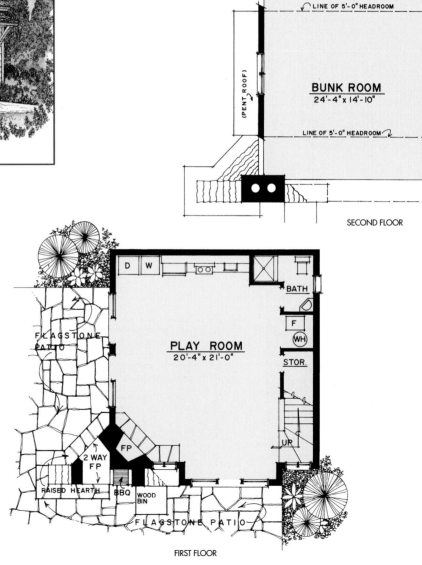

Craftsman stylings grace this two-story bungalow home, designed for a narrow lot. Shingles and siding present a warm welcome; the front porch opens to the dining room and the gathering room, allowing great entertainment options. The kitchen connects to the living areas with a snack bar and works hard with an island and lots of counter space. The master suite is on this level and delights in a very private bath. Two bedrooms on the upper level have private vanities and a shared bath. Extra storage or bonus space is available for future development.

DESIGN HPT9900051

STYLE: BUNGALOW
FIRST FLOOR: 1,392 SQ. FT.
SECOND FLOOR: 708 SQ. FT.
TOTAL: 2,100 SQ. FT.
BEDROOMS: 3
BATHROOMS: 2½
WIDTH: 32' - 0"
DEPTH: 55' - 0"
FOUNDATION: CRAWLSPACE

SEARCH ONLINE @ EPLANS.COM

GARAGE
20'-0" x 22'-0"

MASTER SUITE
13'-4" x 16'-0"

COVERED PORCH

LAUNDRY

KITCHEN
12'-0" x 14'-2"

MASTER BATH

PDR.

W.I.C.

UP

OPT. CABINETS

DINING ROOM
12'-0" x 13'-6"

GATHERING ROOM
19'-4" x 14'-10"

PORCH

FIRST FLOOR

SUITE 3
15'-0" x 13'-6"

W.I.C.

BATH

HALL

DN

UNIF. STOR./ OPT. BONUS
12'-0" x 15'-0"

SUITE 2
13'-0" x 16'-10"

W.I.C.

SECOND FLOOR

BUNGALOW

This simply designed home is distinguished by its two prominent dormers—one facing front and the other on the left side. The dormer to the left boasts a sunburst window, which spills light into the family room. Enter through a large covered porch to a foyer that looks into the family room. Beyond, a vaulted kitchen/nook area is graced with an abundance of windows and rear-door access. The master bedroom is located at the front of the plan, and is graced with a full bath. On the second floor are two additional bedrooms, each with ample closet space.

DESIGN HPT9900052

STYLE: BUNGALOW
FIRST FLOOR: 820 SQ. FT.
SECOND FLOOR: 350 SQ. FT.
TOTAL: 1,170 SQ. FT.
BEDROOMS: 3
BATHROOMS: 2
WIDTH: 37' - 0"
DEPTH: 67' - 0"
FOUNDATION: SLAB

SEARCH ONLINE @ EPLANS.COM

SECOND FLOOR

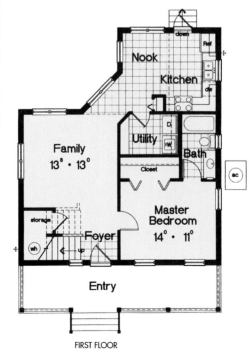

FIRST FLOOR

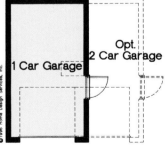

Stone and vertical siding combine to create a memorable exterior for this beautiful bungalow. The front door opens directly to the great room, which boasts a corner fireplace. Nearby, the dining room is conveniently close to the efficient kitchen. A box-bay window highlights the master suite, secluded to the rear of the plan; this suite includes a walk-in closet and a private bath with a luxurious corner tub. Upstairs, two secondary bedrooms—one with a built-in desk—share a full bath.

DESIGN HPT9900053

STYLE: BUNGALOW
FIRST FLOOR: 1,569 SQ. FT.
SECOND FLOOR: 436 SQ. FT.
TOTAL: 2,005 SQ. FT.
BEDROOMS: 3
BATHROOMS: 2½
WIDTH: 44' - 2"
DEPTH: 57' - 6"
FOUNDATION: CRAWLSPACE, SLAB, BASEMENT

SEARCH ONLINE @ EPLANS.COM

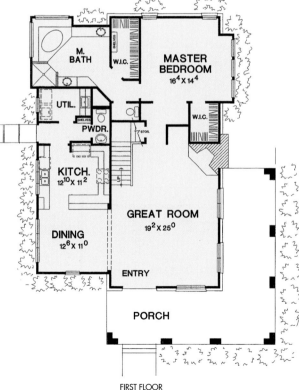

FIRST FLOOR

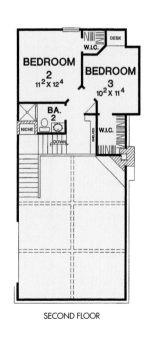

SECOND FLOOR

BUNGALOW

With shuttered arched windows, a flat-top dormer, and a clerestory, this cozy bungalow invites you to nestle in for a long comfortable stay. The great room, with a vaulted ceiling and gas-fueled fireplace, and the dining room, with easy service proximity to the kitchen, highlight the open layout of this plan. The kitchen has ample counter space, a handy pantry, and room for a small desk. Near the entrance is the den, with an option of a built-in media and entertainment center. The master suite enjoys a bath with many lavish comforts, including a spa tub, separate shower, and dual-basin vanity. Another bedroom has access to a hall bath. The two-car garage has additional space for a motorcycle or garden tractor.

DESIGN HPT9900054

STYLE: BUNGALOW
SQUARE FOOTAGE: 1,728
BEDROOMS: 2
BATHROOMS: 2
WIDTH: 55' - 0"
DEPTH: 48' - 0"
FOUNDATION: CRAWLSPACE, BASEMENT

SEARCH ONLINE @ EPLANS.COM

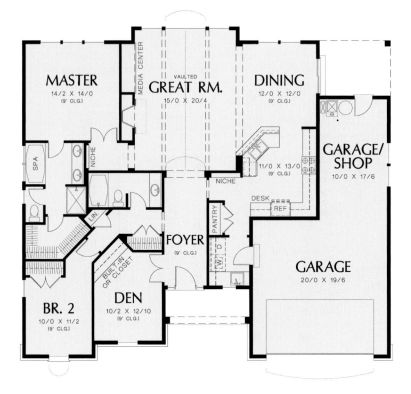

The open layout and special amenities found inside this quaint bungalow will win you over at first sight. The family cook will find the kitchen—with a walk-in pantry, loads of shelves and counters, and a snack bar—much to their liking. The kitchen opens easily into the dining area, which flows into the great room with a rear window wall, fireplace, and built-in entertainment center. The den, with a window overlooking the front porch, can include either a built-in desk or a closet. A vaulted ceiling soars above the bedroom in the master suite; a walk-in closet includes lots of shelf space. Another bedroom features two closets, a cozy window seat, built-in bookshelves, and access to a hall bath.

DESIGN HPT9900055

STYLE: BUNGALOW
SQUARE FOOTAGE: 1,975
BEDROOMS: 2
BATHROOMS: 2
WIDTH: 52' - 0"
DEPTH: 58' - 0"
FOUNDATION: CRAWLSPACE, BASEMENT

SEARCH ONLINE @ EPLANS.COM

BUNGALOW

This charming one-story plan features a facade that is accented by a stone pediment and a shed-dormer window. Inside, elegant touches grace the efficient floor plan. Vaulted ceilings adorn the great room and master bedroom, and a 10-foot tray ceiling highlights the foyer. One of the front bedrooms makes a perfect den; another accesses a full hall bath with a linen closet. The great room, which opens to the porch, includes a fireplace and a media niche. The dining room offers outdoor access and built-ins for ultimate convenience.

DESIGN HPT9900056

STYLE: BUNGALOW
SQUARE FOOTAGE: 1,580
BEDROOMS: 3
BATHROOMS: 2½
WIDTH: 50' - 0"
DEPTH: 48' - 0"
FOUNDATION: CRAWLSPACE, BASEMENT

SEARCH ONLINE @ EPLANS.COM

PORCH

DINING
11/2 X 12/8
(9' CLG.)

SHELVES

VAULTED
MASTER
12/8 X 15/2

VAULTED
GREAT RM.
16/8 X 17/0

BUILT-INS

11/4 X 12/10

REF.

W. D.

P.

MEDIA
LIN. LIN.

FOYER
(10' CLG.)

BR. 3/
DEN
10/6 X 11/4
(9' CLG.)

GARAGE
20/6 X 21/0

BR. 2
11/0 X 10/0
(9' CLG.)

PORCH

© Alan Mascord Design Associates, Inc.

Exterior textured materials and graceful double entry doors create an inviting atmosphere. A gas fireplace and dual sliding glass doors bring warmth and light to the great room and formal dining area; a sloped ceiling crowns the combined rooms. An open bar separates kitchen work areas from the gathering rooms, yet offers convenience to the living spaces. Split bedrooms offer privacy to the master suite, adorned by a tray ceiling and a lavish bath. Creating a library from one of the secondary bedrooms is a popular option and expands the versatility of the plan. A covered rear porch and full basement provide added benefits to this design.

DESIGN HPT9900057

STYLE: BUNGALOW
SQUARE FOOTAGE: 1,651
BEDROOMS: 3
BATHROOMS: 2
WIDTH: 60' - 9"
DEPTH: 49' - 0"
FOUNDATION: BASEMENT

SEARCH ONLINE @ EPLANS.COM

Master Bedroom 12' x 16'2"
Dressing
Porch
Laun.
WALK-IN CLOSET
Hall
Dining Area 12'8" x 13'
SLOPED CEILING
Great Room 16'4" x 16'6"
SLOPED CEILING
Bedroom 11'6" x 10'6"
SLOPED CEILING
Kitchen 13'9" x 11'
Foyer
Bath
Garage 20' x 23'
Porch
Bedroom 11'4" x 10'6"

BUNGALOW

This petite bungalow, perfect for a narrow lot, boasts a charming exterior and a practical floor plan. The front door opens directly to the great room, which offers a fireplace. Just to the left, a short hallway leads to the master suite, with its large walk-in closet and private bath; straight ahead are the kitchen and dining room. Special features here include a walk-in pantry, a built-in niche, and access to a covered rear patio. Two second-floor bedrooms, each with private vanity areas, share a full bath; a nearby built-in desk provides a convenient space for homework.

DESIGN HPT9900058

FIRST FLOOR: 1,297 SQ. FT.
SECOND FLOOR: 618 SQ. FT.
TOTAL: 1,915 SQ. FT.
BEDROOMS: 3
BATHROOMS: 2½
WIDTH: 31' - 10"
DEPTH: 75' - 10"
FOUNDATION: CRAWLSPACE, SLAB, BASEMENT

SEARCH ONLINE @ EPLANS.COM

FIRST FLOOR

SECOND FLOOR

ORDER BLUEPRINTS 24 HOURS, 7 DAYS A WEEK, AT 1-800-521-6797

Wide porch pillars lend Craftsman flair to this tidy stucco bungalow. Inside, the spacious living room features a corner niche and a nearby coat closet. Columns define the formal dining room, located between the living room and kitchen; the kitchen opens to a covered rear patio. All three bedrooms—a master suite and two additional bedrooms—boast walk-in closets. The master suite provides a private bath, and the two secondary bedrooms share a full hall bath. The utility area offers an extra closet for linen storage.

DESIGN HPT9900059

STYLE: BUNGALOW
SQUARE FOOTAGE: 1,468
BEDROOMS: 3
BATHROOMS: 2
WIDTH: 36' - 2"
DEPTH: 55' - 8"
FOUNDATION: CRAWLSPACE, SLAB, BASEMENT

SEARCH ONLINE @ EPLANS.COM

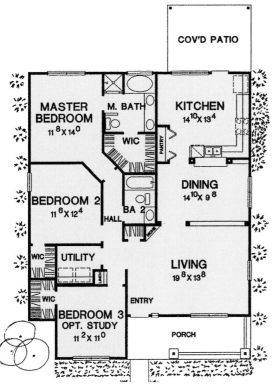

BUNGALOW

A wraparound covered porch is just one of many luxurious touches that fill this bungalow design. Columns add elegance to the entry, living room, and dining room; built-ins and a fireplace enhance the living room. A covered deck and screened porch, accessible from the living room, offer opportunities for outdoor gatherings. Conveniently near the kitchen, a walk-in pantry and butler's pantry allow for easy storage and service. A master suite and two additional bedrooms cluster to the right of the plan; the splendid master bath features a corner tub and shower and a large walk-in closet. Bonus space offers room to grow.

DESIGN HPT9900060

STYLE: BUNGALOW
SQUARE FOOTAGE: 2,405
BONUS SPACE: 375 SQ. FT.
BEDROOMS: 3
BATHROOMS: 2½
WIDTH: 70' - 7"
DEPTH: 89' - 5"
FOUNDATION: CRAWLSPACE, SLAB

SEARCH ONLINE @ EPLANS.COM

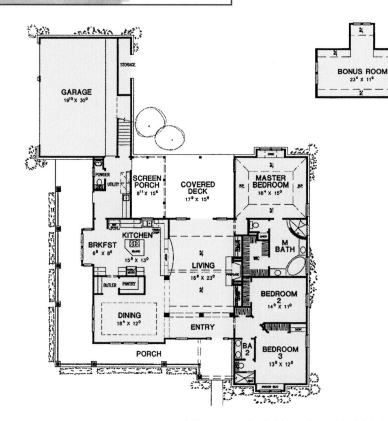

This cozy charmer is very efficient, fitting four bedrooms into just over 1,500 square feet. Gathering spaces include living and dining rooms, separated by columns; the kitchen, brightened by a boxed window, is a sensible, well-designed workspace. Three of the four bedrooms—the master suite and two rear bedrooms— include walk-in closets; the fourth is located right across from a full hall bath. A convenient utility area completes the plan.

Floor plan labels:

- W.I.C.
- BEDROOM 2 — 12² X 11²
- BEDROOM 3 — 11¹⁰ X 11²
- W.I.C.
- HALL
- UTIL.
- BA 2
- LIN.
- BEDROOM 4 — 11¹⁰ X 10⁴
- KITCHEN — 11⁸ X 11⁰
- PAN.
- DINING — 13² X 10⁶
- W.I.C.
- M. BATH
- LIVING — 14⁰ X 16⁰
- MASTER BEDROOM — 15⁰ X 13⁰
- ENTRY
- PORCH

DESIGN HPT9900061

STYLE: BUNGALOW
SQUARE FOOTAGE: 1,553
BEDROOMS: 4
BATHROOMS: 2
WIDTH: 36' - 10"
DEPTH: 57' - 2"
FOUNDATION: CRAWLSPACE, SLAB

SEARCH ONLINE @ EPLANS.COM

BUNGALOW

DESIGN HPT9900062

STYLE: BUNGALOW
FIRST FLOOR: 1,508 SQ. FT.
SECOND FLOOR: 446 SQ. FT.
TOTAL: 1,954 SQ. FT.
BONUS SPACE: 651 SQ. FT.
BEDROOMS: 3
BATHROOMS: 3
WIDTH: 50' - 0"
DEPTH: 50' - 0"
FOUNDATION: CRAWLSPACE, SLAB

SEARCH ONLINE @ EPLANS.COM

This snappy-looking bungalow is roomier than it might appear, and a front wrap-around porch and rear patio extend the usable space. A den and a parlor to either side as you enter offer possibilities for both formal get-togethers and informal conversations. The family room and dining area mesh together under a vaulted ceiling; at one end French doors open onto the patio. An angled snack bar—great for quick breakfasts and late-night munching—separates the kitchen from the dining room. A splendid master suite with a luxuriant private bath and a family bedroom are on the right side of the plan. Upstairs, another bedroom and bath open to a loft overlooking the family and dining rooms.

SECOND FLOOR

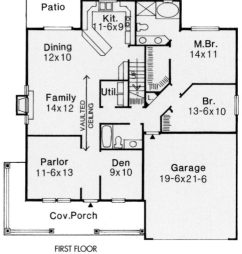

FIRST FLOOR

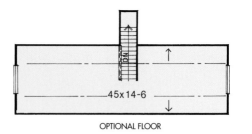

OPTIONAL FLOOR

Columns decorate the covered porch and a dormer accents the rooftop of this classic bungalow home. The foyer leads into the great room, which is warmed by a fireplace. The breakfast room, with sliding glass doors that open to the rear property, brightens the efficient island kitchen. A sitting room is featured in the master suite, along with a spacious walk-in closet and pampering bath. French doors open into the den, which can double as a third bedroom.

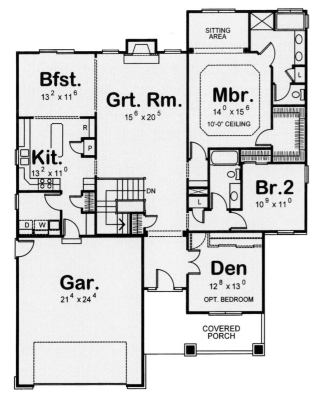

DESIGN HPT9900063

STYLE: BUNGALOW
SQUARE FOOTAGE: 1,902
BEDROOMS: 2
BATHROOMS: 2
WIDTH: 50' - 0"
DEPTH: 62' - 0"

SEARCH ONLINE @ EPLANS.COM

BUNGALOW

A charming shape and amazing natural light mark this well-planned bungalow with comfort and personality. Enter from the covered front porch—two sets of French doors frame the main entrance. The gathering room is presented with a cozy fireplace and opens to the airy dining room. The large kitchen is designed to include a handy breakfast booth. At the rear, a home office (or guest suite) affords plenty of privacy. Upstairs, the master suite delights in an oversized shed dormer window and a vaulted spa bath. An additional bedroom suite completes the plan.

DESIGN HPT9900064

STYLE: BUNGALOW
FIRST FLOOR: 1,061 SQ. FT.
SECOND FLOOR: 914 SQ. FT.
TOTAL: 1,975 SQ. FT.
BEDROOMS: 3
BATHROOMS: 3
WIDTH: 32' - 0"
DEPTH: 45' - 0"
FOUNDATION: CRAWLSPACE

SEARCH ONLINE @ EPLANS.COM

SECOND FLOOR

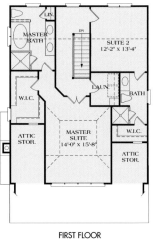

FIRST FLOOR

Cozy living abounds in this comfortable two-story bungalow. Enter the foyer and find a spacious living room with a fireplace to the left. The bayed family room features a fireplace and entry to a screened porch. Upstairs, secondary bedrooms offer ample closet space and direct access to a shared bath. The master suite contains a large walk-in closet, a double-bowl vanity, and a compartmented shower and toilet.

DESIGN HPT9900065

STYLE: BUNGALOW
FIRST FLOOR: 1,482 SQ. FT.
SECOND FLOOR: 885 SQ. FT.
TOTAL: 2,367 SQ. FT.
BEDROOMS: 3
BATHROOMS: 2½
WIDTH: 64' - 0"
DEPTH: 50' - 0"
FOUNDATION: BASEMENT

SEARCH ONLINE @ EPLANS.COM

SECOND FLOOR

FIRST FLOOR

BUNGALOW

Verandas at both the front and rear of this engaging bungalow provide outdoor enthusiasts with a front-row seat to enjoy the changing seasons. To further entice you outdoors, the master bedroom, the breakfast room, and the gathering room all have French doors that open onto the rear veranda. During frosty weather, a raised-hearth fireplace warms the combined gathering room and dining room and offers a friendly invitation. Bedrooms are efficiently separated from the living area. A romantic fireplace and a luxurious private bath enhance the master suite. Two family bedrooms share a full bath. The second floor holds a lounge that makes a great getaway for quiet contemplation or study.

DESIGN HPT9900066

STYLE: BUNGALOW
FIRST FLOOR: 2,918 SQ. FT.
SECOND FLOOR: 330 SQ. FT.
TOTAL: 3,248 SQ. FT.
BEDROOMS: 3
BATHROOMS: 2½
WIDTH: 82' - 8"
DEPTH: 61' - 0"
FOUNDATION: BASEMENT

SEARCH ONLINE @ EPLANS.COM

SECOND FLOOR

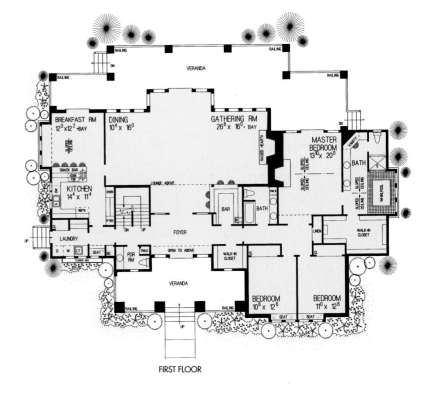

FIRST FLOOR

Details make the difference in this darling two-bedroom—or make it a three-bedroom—bungalow. From the front covered porch to the rear porch with decorative railings and stairs, this home offers a sense of comfortable elegance. A gathering room with a through-fireplace offers wide views to the outdoors, and the formal dining room has its own door to the rear porch. To the front of the plan, a family bedroom has its own full bath, and a secluded study—or guest bedroom—offers space for reading or quiet conversation. Upstairs, the master suite offers a through-fireplace shared with a private bath, space for an audiovisual center, and a roomy walk-in closet.

DESIGN HPT9900067

L D

STYLE: BUNGALOW
FIRST FLOOR: 1,557 SQ. FT.
SECOND FLOOR: 540 SQ. FT.
TOTAL: 2,097 SQ. FT.
BEDROOMS: 2
BATHROOMS: 2
WIDTH: 48' - 0"
DEPTH: 43' - 8"
FOUNDATION: BASEMENT

SEARCH ONLINE @ EPLANS.COM

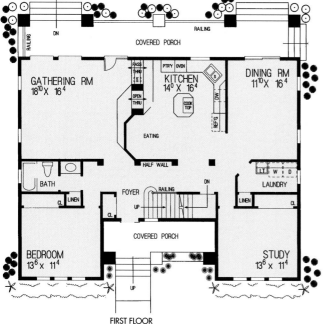

FIRST FLOOR

OPTIONAL LAYOUT

SECOND FLOOR

QUOTE ONE®
Cost to build? See page 123
to order complete cost estimate
to build this house in your area!

BUNGALOW

Little luxuries—a fireplace in the great room, a sauna near the first-floor bath, and a built-in hot tub on the rear deck—make this a memorable bungalow plan. The efficient kitchen features a counter cooktop, with a snack bar that overlooks the great room, and a cozy nook with space for a dining table sits just to the left of the kitchen. Nearby, a large pantry provides extra storage space. The first-floor bedroom easily accesses a hall bath; upstairs, another bedroom includes a sloped ceiling and access to a loft with space for an optional bath.

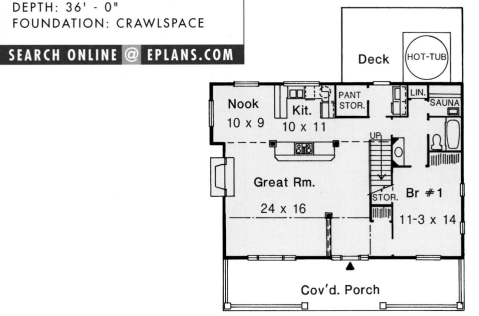

FIRST FLOOR

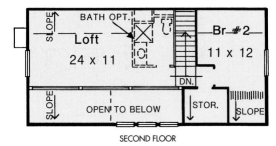

SECOND FLOOR

Craftsman-style windows decorate the facade of this beautiful bungalow design. Inside, the formal dining room, to the left of the foyer, can double as a study; the family room offers a sloping ceiling and a fireplace option. In the breakfast nook, a window seat and sliding glass doors that open to the covered patio provide places to enjoy the outdoors. The master bedroom dominates the right side of the plan, boasting a walk-in closet and private bath. Upstairs, two secondary bedrooms—both with walk-in closets, and one with a private bath—sit to either side of a game room.

DESIGN HPT9900069

STYLE: BUNGALOW
FIRST FLOOR: 1,305 SQ. FT.
SECOND FLOOR: 636 SQ. FT.
TOTAL: 1,941 SQ. FT.
BEDROOMS: 4
BATHROOMS: 2½
WIDTH: 42' - 4"
DEPTH: 46' - 10"
FOUNDATION: CRAWLSPACE, SLAB, BASEMENT

SEARCH ONLINE @ EPLANS.COM

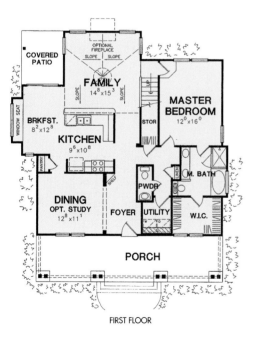

FIRST FLOOR

SECOND FLOOR

BUNGALOW

Contemporary with a country twist, this modern bungalow has it all. Two verandas and a screened porch enlarge the plan and enhance indoor/outdoor livability. The sloped ceiling in the gathering room gives this area an open, airy quality. The breakfast room, with its wealth of windows, will be a cheerful and bright space to enjoy a cup of morning coffee. Added extras provide a thoughtful touch: abundant storage space, walk-in pantry, built-in planning desk, and pass-through snack bar. The master suite features a pampering whirlpool tub to soak your cares away.

DESIGN HPT9900070

L

STYLE: BUNGALOW
SQUARE FOOTAGE: 1,951
BEDROOMS: 3
BATHROOMS: 2
WIDTH: 56' - 0"
DEPTH: 48' - 8"
FOUNDATION: BASEMENT

SEARCH ONLINE @ EPLANS.COM

QUOTE ONE®

Cost to build? See page 123
to order complete cost estimate
to build this house in your area!

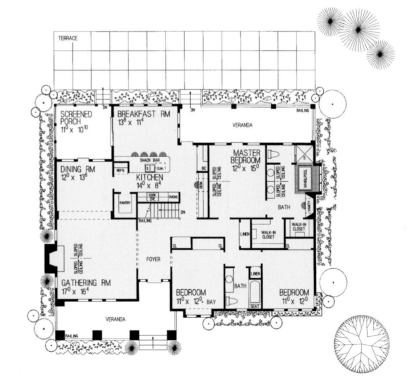

ORDER BLUEPRINTS 24 HOURS, 7 DAYS A WEEK, AT 1-800-521-6797

This handsome bungalow breathes comfort—from the stately columns framing the front covered porch to the family-friendly interior. Step into the foyer fitted with a niche for statuary, and either turn left into the elegant dining room or go straight ahead into the wide open space of the family room. At the far end, a warming fireplace is flanked on both sides by French doors graced with transom windows. An angled serving bar links this room with the kitchen and breakfast alcove. The luxuriant master suite fills the entire left wing. A coffered ceiling rests above the bedchamber; a vaulted ceiling tops the bath. A huge walk-in closet, His and Hers vanities, a shower with a seat, and radius transom windows overlooking a garden tub highlight the comforts found here. On the other side of the house, two family bedrooms enjoy walk-in closets and share a bath.

DESIGN HPT9900071

STYLE: BUNGALOW
SQUARE FOOTAGE: 2,073
BONUS SPACE: 350 SQ. FT.
BEDROOMS: 3
BATHROOMS: 2½
WIDTH: 59' - 0"
DEPTH: 57' - 0"
FOUNDATION: CRAWLSPACE, BASEMENT

SEARCH ONLINE @ EPLANS.COM

BUNGALOW

This fine bungalow, with its multiple gables, rafter tails, and pillared front porch, will be the envy of any neighborhood. A beam-ceilinged great room is further enhanced by a through-fireplace and French doors to the rear terrace. The U-shaped kitchen features a cooktop island with a snack bar and offers a beam-ceilinged breakfast/keeping room that shares the through-fireplace with the great room. Two secondary bedrooms share a full bath; the master suite is designed to pamper. Here, the homeowner will be pleased with a walk-in closet, a separate shower, and access to the terrace. The two-car garage has a side entrance and will easily shelter the family fleet.

DESIGN HPT9900072

STYLE: BUNGALOW
SQUARE FOOTAGE: 2,489
BEDROOMS: 3
BATHROOMS: 2½
WIDTH: 68' - 3"
DEPTH: 62' - 0"
FOUNDATION: WALKOUT BASEMENT

SEARCH ONLINE @ EPLANS.COM

Cozy and completely functional, this 1½-story bungalow has many amenities not often found in homes its size. To the left of the foyer is a media room, and to the rear is the gathering room with a fireplace. Attached to the gathering room is a formal dining room with rear-terrace access. The kitchen features a curved casual eating area and island workstation. The right side of the first floor is dominated by the master suite, which offers access to the rear terrace and a luxurious bath. Upstairs are two family bedrooms connected by a loft area overlooking the gathering room and foyer.

DESIGN HPT9900073

LD

STYLE: BUNGALOW
FIRST FLOOR: 1,636 SQ. FT.
SECOND FLOOR: 572 SQ. FT.
TOTAL: 2,208 SQ. FT.
BEDROOMS: 3
BATHROOMS: 2½
WIDTH: 52' - 0"
DEPTH: 46' - 2"
FOUNDATION: BASEMENT

SEARCH ONLINE @ EPLANS.COM

QUOTE ONE®
Cost to build? See page 123
to order complete cost estimate
to build this house in your area!

FIRST FLOOR

SECOND FLOOR

BUNGALOW

This rustic stone and siding bungalow with Craftsman influences includes a multitude of windows flooding the interior with natural light. The foyer opens to the great room, which is complete with three sets of French doors and a two-sided fireplace. The master suite offers an expansive private bath, two large walk-in closets, a bay window, and a tray ceiling. The dining room, kitchen, and utility room make an efficient trio.

DESIGN HPT9900074

STYLE: BUNGALOW
FIRST FLOOR: 1,798 SQ. FT.
SECOND FLOOR: 900 SQ. FT.
TOTAL: 2,698 SQ. FT.
BEDROOMS: 3
BATHROOMS: 3
WIDTH: 54' - 0"
DEPTH: 57' - 0"
FOUNDATION: CRAWLSPACE

SEARCH ONLINE @ EPLANS.COM

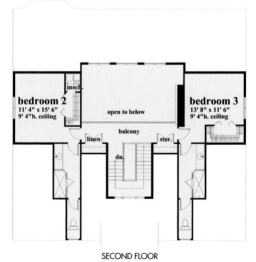

SECOND FLOOR

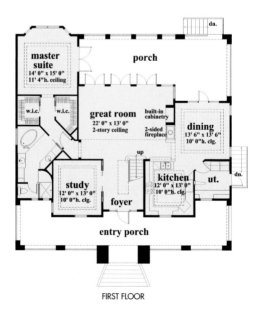

FIRST FLOOR

With a rugged blend of stone and siding, an inviting mix of details creates the kind of comfortable beauty that every homeowner craves. Massive stone columns support a striking pediment entry. A spacious formal dining room complements a gourmet kitchen designed to serve any occasion and equipped with a walk-in pantry and a nearby powder room. The morning nook boasts a wall of glass that allows casual diners to kick back and be at one with nature. Separate sleeping quarters thoughtfully place the master suite to the right of the plan, in a wing of the home that includes a private porch. Guest suites on the opposite side of the plan share a hall and a staircase that leads to a lower-level mudroom, porch, and ski storage.

DESIGN HPT9900075

STYLE: BUNGALOW
SQUARE FOOTAGE: 2,430
BEDROOMS: 3
BATHROOMS: 3
WIDTH: 70' - 2"
DEPTH: 53' - 0"
FOUNDATION: BASEMENT

SEARCH ONLINE @ EPLANS.COM

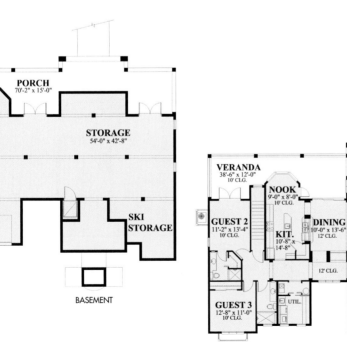

PRAIRIE

This three-bedroom home, though smaller than standard Prairie-style designs, shows a definite Prairie influence. A stairway in the great room leads to the lower level and is open to the two-story rear windows. A three-sided stone fireplace brings warmth and light to the spacious island kitchen, breakfast area, and great room. Depending on the need, a den or dining room is located just to the right of the entryway. The master suite provides ample closet space and a whirlpool tub. Separated from the master wing for privacy, two secondary bedrooms share a full bath.

DESIGN HPT9900076

STYLE: PRAIRIE
SQUARE FOOTAGE: 2,167
BEDROOMS: 3
BATHROOMS: 2
WIDTH: 55' - 4"
DEPTH: 61' - 4"

SEARCH ONLINE @ EPLANS.COM

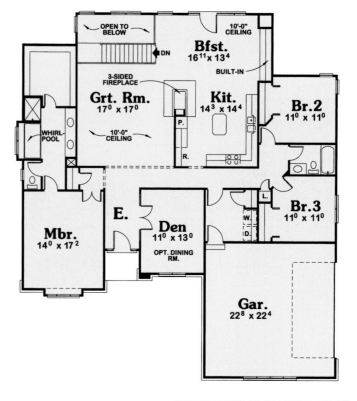

A discreet Prairie style is celebrated on the facade of this lovely design. A see-through fireplace connects the great room and the breakfast area. The formal dining room offers fabulous interior vistas that extend to the rear propery. A central staircase leads up to a landing with double doors opening to the master suite. This suite features barrel-vaulted ceilings and an oval whirlpool tub. On the second floor, a computer loft with a built-in desk overlooks the stunning great room. Three family bedrooms share a full bath.

DESIGN HPT9900077

STYLE: PRAIRIE
FIRST FLOOR: 1,735 SQ. FT.
SECOND FLOOR: 841 SQ. FT.
TOTAL: 2,576 SQ. FT.
BEDROOMS: 4
BATHROOMS: 2½
WIDTH: 58' - 8"
DEPTH: 54' - 0"

SEARCH ONLINE @ EPLANS.COM

FIRST FLOOR

SECOND FLOOR

PRAIRIE

With a low-pitched hipped roof and symmetrical facade, this design serves as a fine example of an American Foursquare home, one of the earliest Prairie-style designs. Its simple floor plan begins with formal rooms—the dining room and living room/study—to either side of the foyer. Next, the kitchen/breakfast area flows gracefully into the family room, which includes a fireplace and built-in shelves and opens to a covered patio. The master suite boasts two walk-in closets and a private bath; upstairs, three bedrooms—all with walk-in closets—join a game room.

DESIGN HPT9900078

STYLE: PRAIRIE
FIRST FLOOR: 1,742 SQ. FT.
SECOND FLOOR: 958 SQ. FT.
TOTAL: 2,700 SQ. FT.
BEDROOMS: 4
BATHROOMS: 3½
WIDTH: 38' - 7"
DEPTH: 96' - 3"
FOUNDATION: CRAWLSPACE,
SLAB, BASEMENT

SEARCH ONLINE @ EPLANS.COM

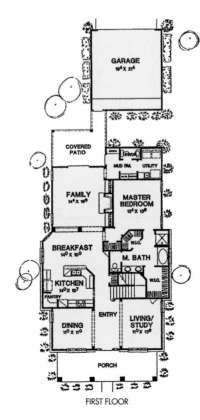

FIRST FLOOR

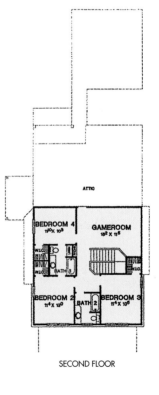

SECOND FLOOR

Tall windows in every room bring plenty of natural light into this Prairie design, and a wide, covered front porch provides a place to enjoy the outdoors. The dining room, to the right of the entry, is conveniently close to the kitchen, which includes a pantry and a niche. Nearby, the breakfast area opens to the rear patio, and the spacious family room is a comfortable gathering spot. Upstairs, the elegant master suite features a private bath and a walk-in closet with built-in shelves; two additonal bedrooms share a full bath.

DESIGN HPT9900079

STYLE: PRAIRIE
FIRST FLOOR: 1,217 SQ. FT.
SECOND FLOOR: 1,057 SQ. FT.
TOTAL: 2,274 SQ. FT.
BEDROOMS: 3
BATHROOMS: 2½
WIDTH: 38' - 0"
DEPTH: 40' - 5"
FOUNDATION: CRAWLSPACE, SLAB, BASEMENT

SEARCH ONLINE @ EPLANS.COM

PATIO

BRKFST.
11⁴ X 12⁸

KITCHEN
10⁰ X 12⁸

FAMILY
16⁰ X 17⁴

PANTRY

REF. SPACE

STORAGE

POWDER

UTILITY

STUDY
14⁸ X 12⁴

DINING
13⁸ X 10⁸

ENTRY

PORCH

FIRST FLOOR

MASTER BEDROOM
13⁴ X 14⁸

GAME ROOM
11⁰ X 12⁸

BEDROOM 3
11⁸ X 10⁸

LINEN

M BATH

BA 2

WIC

WIC

WIC

SHELVES

OPEN TO BELOW

BEDROOM 2
13⁸ X 10⁰

SECOND FLOOR

PRAIRIE

DESIGN HPT9900080

STYLE: PRAIRIE
FIRST FLOOR: 3,253 SQ. FT.
SECOND FLOOR: 1,747 SQ. FT.
TOTAL: 5,000 SQ. FT.
BEDROOMS: 5
BATHROOMS: 5½
WIDTH: 112' - 9"
DEPTH: 89' - 10"
FOUNDATION: CRAWLSPACE

SEARCH ONLINE @ EPLANS.COM

This impressive two-story Prairie-style design features a modern layout filled with abundant rooms and amenities. A wide front porch welcomes you inside to an entry flanked on either side by formal living and dining rooms. Built-ins enhance the dining room, and the living room shares a see-through fireplace with the library/study. The island kitchen offers a utility room and food pantry nearby, while it overlooks the breakfast and family rooms. The mudroom accesses the rear porch and sunroom. The luxurious master suite contains a sitting area, His and Hers walk-in closets, a private bath, and an exercise room. At the rear, planters enhance the raised patio area. The second floor features three additional bedrooms. A study between Bedrooms 3 and 4 is perfect for the kids. A game room, sleep loft, and rear balcony complete this floor.

SECOND FLOOR

FIRST FLOOR

ORDER BLUEPRINTS 24 HOURS, 7 DAYS A WEEK, AT 1-800-521-6797

A great room with a fireplace, tall double windows, and access to a covered rear porch is the highlight of this lovely Prairie-style home. The kitchen—with a walk-in pantry, central island, and plenty of counter space—easily serves the formal dining room. The study, which features a walk-in closet and adjoins a full bath, could serve as a bedroom if neccessary. Upstairs, the master bedroom boasts a full bath with a spa tub and a shower with a built-in seat. Two additional bedrooms share a full bath that includes a linen closet.

DESIGN HPT9900081

STYLE: PRAIRIE
FIRST FLOOR: 1,290 SQ. FT.
SECOND FLOOR: 1,132 SQ. FT.
TOTAL: 2,422 SQ. FT.
BEDROOMS: 3
BATHROOMS: 3
WIDTH: 35' - 11"
DEPTH: 51' - 5"
FOUNDATION: CRAWLSPACE, SLAB

SEARCH ONLINE @ EPLANS.COM

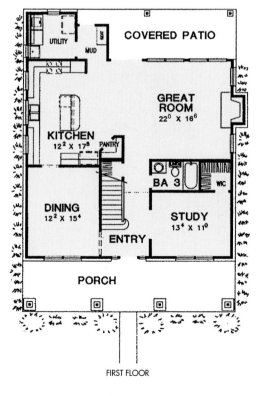

FIRST FLOOR

SECOND FLOOR

PRAIRIE

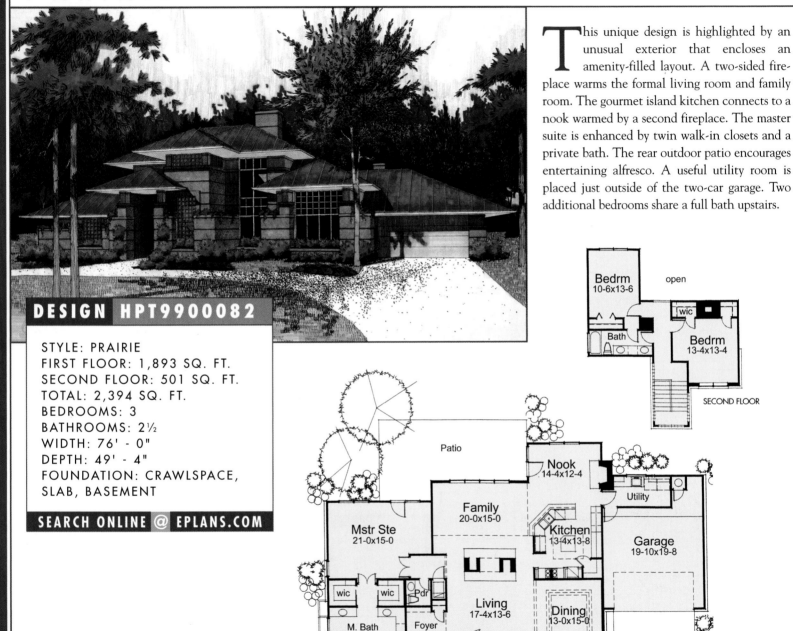

This unique design is highlighted by an unusual exterior that encloses an amenity-filled layout. A two-sided fireplace warms the formal living room and family room. The gourmet island kitchen connects to a nook warmed by a second fireplace. The master suite is enhanced by twin walk-in closets and a private bath. The rear outdoor patio encourages entertaining alfresco. A useful utility room is placed just outside of the two-car garage. Two additional bedrooms share a full bath upstairs.

DESIGN HPT9900082

STYLE: PRAIRIE
FIRST FLOOR: 1,893 SQ. FT.
SECOND FLOOR: 501 SQ. FT.
TOTAL: 2,394 SQ. FT.
BEDROOMS: 3
BATHROOMS: 2½
WIDTH: 76' - 0"
DEPTH: 49' - 4"
FOUNDATION: CRAWLSPACE, SLAB, BASEMENT

SEARCH ONLINE @ EPLANS.COM

This fascinating Prairie-style home enjoys two balcony-style decks and a master suite that takes up the whole second floor. The great room, dining area, and kitchen are joined together in a flexible and aesthetically pleasing open layout. French doors lead to both decks from the great room, warmed by a cozy fireplace. Two family bedrooms both have direct access to the same bath. Upstairs, the resplendent master suite reigns. A three-car garage, a workshop, and loads of unfinished storage space are located on the basement level.

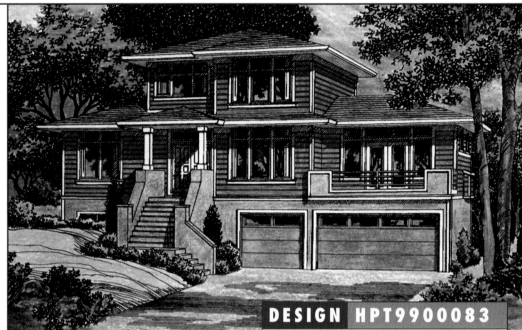

DESIGN HPT9900083

STYLE: PRAIRIE
FIRST FLOOR: 1,538 SQ. FT.
SECOND FLOOR: 628 SQ. FT.
TOTAL: 2,166 SQ. FT.
BEDROOMS: 3
BATHROOMS: 2½
WIDTH: 53' - 0"
DEPTH: 35' - 0"
FOUNDATION: CRAWLSPACE, BASEMENT

SEARCH ONLINE @ EPLANS.COM

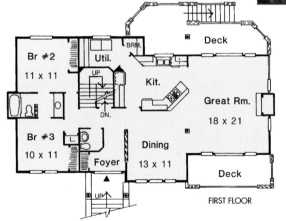

FIRST FLOOR

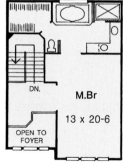

SECOND FLOOR

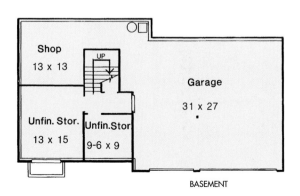

BASEMENT

PRAIRIE

Frank Lloyd Wright had a knack for enhancing the environment with the homes he designed. This adaptation reflects his purest Prairie style complemented by a brick exterior, a multitude of windows, and a low-slung hipped roof. The foyer introduces a gallery wall to display your artwork. To the right, an archway leads to a formal dining room lined with a wall of windows. Nearby, the spacious kitchen features an island snack bar. The two-story family/great room provides an ideal setting for formal or informal gatherings. If philosophical discussions heat up, they can be continued in the open courtyard. The left wing contains the sleeping quarters and an office/den. The private master suite includes a sitting area, a walk-in closet, and a lavish master bath.

DESIGN HPT9900084

L

STYLE: PRAIRIE
SQUARE FOOTAGE: 2,626
BEDROOMS: 3
BATHROOMS: 2½
WIDTH: 75' - 10"
DEPTH: 69' - 4"
FOUNDATION: CRAWLSPACE

SEARCH ONLINE @ EPLANS.COM

QUOTE ONE®

Cost to build? See page 123
to order complete cost estimate
to build this house in your area!

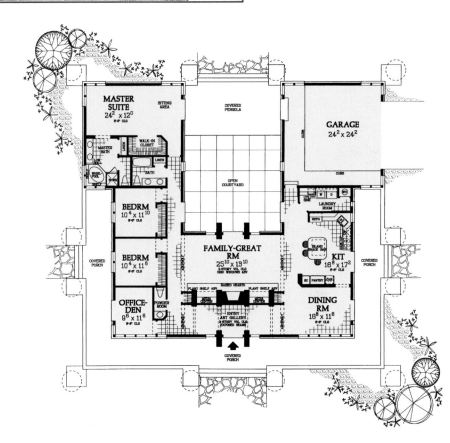

Form follows function as dual gallery halls lead from formal areas to split sleeping quarters in this Prairie adaptation. At the heart of the plan, the grand-scale great room offers a raised-hearth fireplace framed by built-in cabinetry and plant shelves. Open planning combines the country kitchen with an informal dining space and adds an island counter with a snack bar. A lavish master suite harbors a sitting area with private access to the covered pergola. The secondary sleeping wing includes a spacious guest suite. A fifth bedroom or home office offers its own door to the wraparound porch.

DESIGN HPT9900085

L

STYLE: PRAIRIE
SQUARE FOOTAGE: 3,278
BEDROOMS: 4
BATHROOMS: 3½
WIDTH: 75' - 10"
DEPTH: 69' - 4"
FOUNDATION: CRAWLSPACE

SEARCH ONLINE @ EPLANS.COM

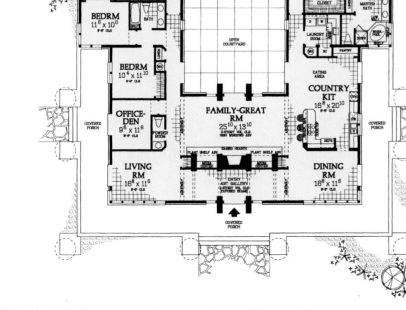

QUOTE ONE®
Cost to build? See page 123
to order complete cost estimate
to build this house in your area!

PRAIRIE

This exquisite brick-and-stucco contemporary home takes its cue from the tradition of Frank Lloyd Wright. The formal living and dining areas combine to provide a spectacular view of the rear grounds. "Unique" best describes the private master suite, highlighted by a multitude of amenities. The family living area encompasses the left portion of the plan, featuring a spacious family room with a corner fireplace, access to the covered patio from the breakfast area, and a step-saving kitchen. Bedroom 2 connects to a private bath. Upstairs, two bedrooms share a balcony, a sitting room, and a full bath.

DESIGN HPT9900086

STYLE: PRAIRIE
FIRST FLOOR: 2,531 SQ. FT.
SECOND FLOOR: 669 SQ. FT.
TOTAL: 3,200 SQ. FT.
BEDROOMS: 4
BATHROOMS: 3½ + ½
WIDTH: 82' - 4"
DEPTH: 72' - 0"
FOUNDATION: SLAB

SEARCH ONLINE @ EPLANS.COM

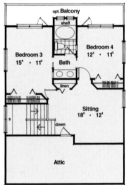

SECOND FLOOR

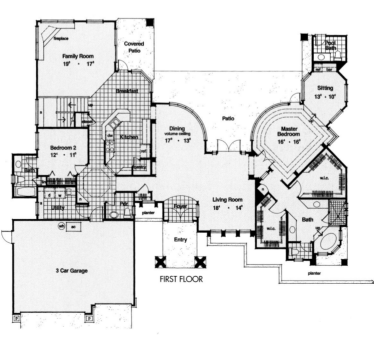

FIRST FLOOR

eplans.com

THE GATEWAY
TO YOUR NEW HOME

Looking for more plans? Got questions?
Try our one-stop home plans resource—eplans.com.

We'll help you streamline the plan selection process, so your dreams can become reality faster than you ever imagined. From choosing your home plan and ideal location to finding an experienced contractor, eplans.com will guide you every step of the way.

Mix and match! Explore! At eplans.com you can combine all your top criteria to find your perfect match. Search for your ideal home plan by any or all of the following:
> Number of bedrooms or baths,
> Total square feet,
> House style,
> Designer, and
> Cost.

With over 10,000 plans, the options are endless. Colonial, ranch, country, and Victorian are just a few of the house styles offered. Keep in mind your essential lifestyle features—whether to include a porch, fireplace, bonus room or main floor laundry room. And the garage—how many cars must it accommodate, if any? By filling out the preference page on eplans.com, we'll help you narrow your search. And, don't forget to enjoy a virtual home tour before any decisions are set in stone.

At eplans.com we'll make the building process a snap to understand. At the click of a button you'll find a complete building guide. And our eplan task planner will create a construction calendar just for you. Here you'll find links to tips and other valuable information to help you every step of the way—from choosing a site to moving day.

For your added convenience, our home plans experts are available for live, one-on-one chats at eplans.com. Building a home may seem like a complicated project, but it doesn't have to be—particularly if you'll let us help you from start to finish.

COPYRIGHT
DOS & DON'TS

Blueprints for residential construction (or working drawings, as they are often called in the industry) are copyrighted intellectual property, protected under the terms of United States Copyright Law and, therefore, cannot be copied legally for use in building. However, we've made it easy for you to get what you need to build your home, without violating copyright law. Following are some guidelines to help you obtain the right number of copies for your chosen blueprint design.

COPYRIGHT DO

■ Do purchase enough copies of the blueprints to satisfy building requirements. As a rule for a home or project plan, you will need a set for yourself, two or three for your builder and subcontractors, two for the local building department, and one to three for your mortgage lender. You may want to check with your local building department or your builder to see how many they need before you purchase. You may need to buy eight to 10 sets; note that some areas of the country require purchase of vellums (also called reproducibles) instead of blueprints. Vellums can be written on and changed more easily than blueprints. Also, remember, plans are only good for one-time construction.

■ Do consider reverse blueprints if you want to flop the plan. Lettering and numbering will appear backward, but the reversed sets will help you and your builder better visualize the design.

■ Do take advantage of multiple-set discounts at the time you place your order. Usually, purchasing additional sets after you receive your initial order is not as cost-effective.

■ Do take advantage of vellums. Though they are a little more expensive, they can be changed, copied, and used for one-time construction of a home. You will receive a copyright release letter with your vellums that will allow you to have them copied.

■ Do talk with one of our professional service representatives before placing your order. They can give you great advice about what packages are available for your chosen design and what will work best for your particular situation.

COPYRIGHT DON'T

■ Don't think you should purchase only one set of blueprints for a building project. One is fine if you want to study the plan closely, but will not be enough for actual building.

■ Don't expect your builder or a copy center to make copies of standard blueprints. They cannot legally—most copy centers are aware of this.

■ Don't purchase standard blueprints if you know you'll want to make changes to the plans; vellums are a better value.

■ Don't use blueprints or vellums more than one time. Additional fees apply if you want to build more than one time from a set of drawings. ■

hanley ▲ wood
HomePlanners
ORDERING IS EASY

HANLEY WOOD HOMEPLANNERS HAS EVERYTHING YOU NEED TO BUILD the home of your dreams, and with more than 50 years of experience in the industry, we make it as easy as possible for you to reach those goals. Just follow the steps on these pages and you'll receive a high-quality, ready-to-build set of home blueprints, plus everything else you need to make your home-building effort a success.

WHERE TO BEGIN?
1. CHOOSE YOUR PLAN

■ Browsing magazines, books, and eplans.com can be an exciting and rewarding part of the home-building process. As you search, make a list of the things you want in your dream home—everything from number of bedrooms and baths to details like fireplaces or a home office.

■ Take the time to consider your lot and your neighborhood, and how the home you choose will fit with both. And think about the future—how might your needs change if you plan to live in this house for five, 10, or 20 years?

■ With thousands of plans available, chances are that you'll have no trouble discovering your dream home. If you find something that's almost perfect, our Customization Program can help make it exactly what you want.

■ Most important, be sure to enjoy the process of picking out your new home!

WHAT YOU'LL GET WITH YOUR ORDER

Each designer's blueprint set is unique, but they all provide everything you'll need to build your home. Here are some standard elements you can expect to find in your plans:

1. FRONT PERSPECTIVE
This artist's sketch of the exterior of the house gives you an idea of how the house will look when built and landscaped.

2. FOUNDATION PLANS
This sheet shows the foundation layout including support walls, excavated and unexcavated areas, if any, and foundation notes. If your plan features slab construction rather than a basement, the plan shows footings and details for a monolithic slab. This page, or another in the set, may include a sample plot plan for locating your house on a building site.

3. DETAILED FLOOR PLANS
These plans show the layout of each floor of the house. Rooms and interior spaces are carefully dimensioned and keys are given for cross-section details provided later in the plans. The positions of electrical outlets and switches are shown.

4. HOUSE CROSS-SECTIONS
Large-scale views show sections or cutaways of the foundation, interior walls, exterior walls, floors, stairways, and roof details. Additional cross-sections may show important changes in floor, ceiling, or roof heights, or the relationship of one level to another. Extremely valuable during construction, these sections show exactly how the various parts of the house fit together.

5. INTERIOR ELEVATIONS
These elevations, or drawings, show the design and placement of kitchen and bathroom cabinets, laundry areas, fireplaces, bookcases, and other built-ins. Little extras, such as mantelpiece and wainscoting drawings, plus molding sections, provide details that give your home that custom touch.

6. EXTERIOR ELEVATIONS
Every blueprint set comes with drawings of the front exterior, and may include the rear and sides of your house as well. These drawings give necessary notes on exterior materials and finishes. Particular attention is given to cornice detail, brick, and stone accents or other finish items that make your home unique.

HANLEY WOOD HOMEPLANNERS ADVANTAGE
ORDER 24 HOURS!
1-800-521-6797

GETTING DOWN TO BUSINESS
2. PRICE YOUR PLAN

BLUEPRINT PRICE SCHEDULE

PRICE TIERS	1-SET STUDY PACKAGE	4-SET BUILDING PACKAGE	8-SET BUILDING PACKAGE	1-SET REPRODUCIBLE*
P1	$20	$50	$90	$140
P2	$40	$70	$110	$160
P3	$70	$100	$140	$190
P4	$100	$130	$170	$220
P5	$140	$170	$210	$270
P6	$180	$210	$250	$310
A1	$440	$490	$540	$660
A2	$480	$530	$580	$720
A3	$530	$590	$650	$800
A4	$575	$645	$705	$870
C1	$625	$695	$755	$935
C2	$670	$740	$800	$1000
C3	$715	$790	$855	$1075
C4	$765	$840	$905	$1150
L1	$870	$965	$1050	$1300
L2	$945	$1040	$1125	$1420
L3	$1050	$1150	$1240	$1575
L4	$1155	$1260	$1355	$1735
SQ1				.35/SQ. FT.

PRICES SUBJECT TO CHANGE   * REQUIRES A FAX NUMBER

plan #
READY TO ORDER

Once you've found your plan, get your plan number and turn to the following pages to find its price tier. Use the corresponding code and the Blueprint Price Schedule above to determine your price for a variety of blueprint packages.

Keep in mind that you'll need multiple sets to fulfill building requirements, and only reproducible sets may be altered or duplicated.

To the right you'll find prices for additional and reverse blueprint sets. Also note in the following pages whether your home has a corresponding Deck or Landscape Plan, and whether you can order our Quote One® cost-to-build information or a Materials List for your plan.

IT'S EASY TO ORDER
JUST VISIT EPLANS.COM OR CALL
TOLL-FREE
1-800-521-6797

PRICE SCHEDULE FOR ADDITIONAL OPTIONS

OPTIONS FOR PLANS IN TIERS P1-P6	COSTS
ADDITIONAL IDENTICAL BLUEPRINTS FOR "P1-P6" PLANS	$10 PER SET
REVERSE BLUEPRINTS (MIRROR IMAGE) FOR "P1-P6" PLANS	$10 FEE PER ORDER
1 SET OF DECK CONSTRUCTION DETAILS	$14.95 EACH
DECK CONSTRUCTION PACKAGE (INCLUDES 1 SET OF "P1-P6" PLANS, PLUS 1 SET STANDARD DECK CONSTRUCTION DETAILS)	ADD $10 TO BUILDING PACKAGE PRICE
OPTIONS FOR PLANS IN TIERS A1-SQ1	COSTS
ADDITIONAL IDENTICAL BLUEPRINTS IN SAME ORDER FOR "A1-L4" PLANS	$50 PER SET
REVERSE BLUEPRINTS (MIRROR IMAGE) WITH 4- OR 8-SET ORDER FOR "A1-L4" PLANS	$50 FEE PER ORDER
SPECIFICATION OUTLINES	$10 EACH
MATERIALS LISTS FOR "A1-SQ1" PLANS	$70 EACH
IMPORTANT EXTRAS	COSTS
ELECTRICAL, PLUMBING, CONSTRUCTION, AND MECHANICAL DETAIL SETS	$14.95 EACH; ANY TWO $22.95; ANY THREE $29.95; ALL FOUR $39.95
HOME FURNITURE PLANNER	$15.95 EACH
REAR ELEVATION	$10 EACH
QUOTE ONE® SUMMARY COST REPORT	$29.95
QUOTE ONE® DETAILED COST ESTIMATE (FOR MORE DETAILS ABOUT QUOTE ONE®, SEE STEP 3.)	$60

IMPORTANT NOTE
■ THE 1-SET STUDY PACKAGE IS MARKED "NOT FOR CONSTRUCTION."

Source Key
HPT99

PLAN #	PRICE TIER	PAGE	MATERIALS LIST	QUOTE ONE®	DECK	DECK PRICE	LANDSCAPE	LANDSCAPE PRICE	REGIONS
HPT9900002	C1	24							
HPT9900001	C4	29	Y						
HPT9900003	SQ1	33							
HPT9900004	A3	34	Y						
HPT9900005	C3	35							
HPT9900007	A4	37							
HPT9900008	C4	38							
HPT9900009	C2	39	Y	Y	ODA012	P3	OLA084	P3	12345678
HPT9900010	C2	40	Y						
HPT9900011	C3	41							
HPT9900012	C2	42	Y						
HPT9900013	C2	43							
HPT9900014	C2	44							
HPT9900015	C2	45							
HPT9900016	C3	46							
HPT9900017	C2	47							
HPT9900018	C3	48							
HPT9900019	C3	49							
HPT9900020	C3	50							
HPT9900021	C3	51							
HPT9900022	A3	52	Y						
HPT9900023	C1	53	Y						
HPT9900024	C1	54							
HPT9900025	C2	55	Y	Y					
HPT9900026	A4	56	Y						
HPT9900027	A4	57	Y	Y					
HPT9900028	A3	58							

PLAN #	PRICE TIER	PAGE	MATERIALS LIST	QUOTE ONE®	DECK	DECK PRICE	LANDSCAPE	LANDSCAPE PRICE	REGIONS
HPT9900029	A4	59	Y						
HPT9900030	C1	60							
HPT9900031	C1	61							
HPT9900032	C1	62	Y						
HPT9900033	C2	63							
HPT9900034	A3	64	Y						
HPT9900035	A3	65							
HPT9900036	A4	66							
HPT9900037	A4	67							
HPT9900038	A3	68							
HPT9900039	A4	69							
HPT9900040	C1	70							
HPT9900041	A3	71	Y						
HPT9900042	C1	72							
HPT9900043	A3	73	Y	Y			OLA003	P3	123568
HPT9900044	A3	74							
HPT9900045	A4	75							
HPT9900046	C2	76	Y	Y					
HPT9900047	C2	77	Y	Y			OLA003	P3	123568
HPT9900048	C1	78							
HPT9900049	C1	79							
HPT9900050	A2	80							
HPT9900051	C2	81							
HPT9900052	A2	82							
HPT9900053	A4	83							
HPT9900054	A3	84	Y						
HPT9900055	A3	85	Y						

PLAN #	PRICE TIER	PAGE	MATERIALS LIST	QUOTE ONE®	DECK	DECK PRICE	LANDSCAPE	LANDSCAPE PRICE	REGIONS
HPT9900056	A3	86	Y						
HPT9900057	A3	87							
HPT9900058	A3	88							
HPT9900059	A2	89							
HPT9900060	A4	90							
HPT9900061	A3	91							
HPT9900062	A3	92							
HPT9900063	C1	93							
HPT9900064	C1	94							
HPT9900065	C2	95	Y	Y			OLA001	P3	123568
HPT9900066	C4	96	Y	Y			OLA001	P3	123568
HPT9900067	A4	97	Y	Y	ODA012	P3	OLA003	P3	123568
HPT9900068	A3	98							
HPT9900069	A3	99							
HPT9900070	A4	100	Y	Y			OLA001	P3	123568
HPT9900071	C2	101							
HPT9900072	A4	102							
HPT9900073	A4	103	Y	Y	ODA017	P2	OLA010	P3	1234568
HPT9900074	C3	104							
HPT9900075	C1	105							
HPT9900076	A4	106	Y						
HPT9900077	C1	107	Y						
HPT9900078	C1	108							
HPT9900079	A4	109							
HPT9900080	SQ1	110							
HPT9900081	A4	111							
HPT9900082	A4	112							

PLAN #	PRICE TIER	PAGE	MATERIALS LIST	QUOTE ONE®	DECK	DECK PRICE	LANDSCAPE	LANDSCAPE PRICE	REGIONS
HPT9900083	A4	113							
HPT9900084	C2	114	Y	Y			OLA039	P3	347
HPT9900085	C3	115	Y	Y			OLA036	P4	12356
HPT9900086	C3	116							
HPT9900087	C3	36							

WE OFFER A VARIETY OF USEFUL TOOLS THAT CAN HELP YOU THROUGH EVERY STEP OF THE HOME-BUILDING process. From our Materials List to our Customization Program, these items let you put our experience to work for you to ensure that you get exactly what you want out of your dream house.

MATERIALS LIST

For many of the designs in our portfolio, we offer a customized list of materials that helps you plan and estimate the cost of your new home. The Materials List outlines the quantity, type, and size of materials needed to build your house (with the exception of mechanical system items). Included are framing lumber, windows and doors, kitchen and bath cabinetry, rough and finished hardware, and much more. This handy list helps you or your builder cost out materials and serves as a reference sheet when you're compiling bids.

SPECIFICATION OUTLINE

This valuable 16-page document can play an important role in the construction of your house. Fill it in with your builder, and you'll have a step-by-step chronicle of 166 stages or items crucial to the building process. It provides a comprehensive review of the construction process and helps you choose materials.

QUOTE ONE®

The Quote One® system, which helps estimate the cost of building select designs in your zip code, is available in two parts: the Summary Cost Report and the Material Cost Report.

The Summary Cost Report, the first element in the package, breaks down the cost of your home into various categories based on building materials, labor, and installation, and includes three grades of construction: Budget, Standard, and Custom. Make even more informed decisions about your project with the second element of our package, the Material Cost Report. The material and installation cost is shown for each of more than 1,000 line items provided in the standard-grade Materials List, which is included with this tool. Additional space is included for estimates from contractors and subcontractors, such as for mechanical materials, which are not included in our packages.

If you are interested in a plan that does not indicate the availability of Quote One®, please call and ask our sales representatives, who can verify the status for you.

CUSTOMIZATION PROGRAM

If the plan you love needs something changed to make it perfect, our customization experts will ensure that you get nothing less than your dream home. Purchase a reproducible set of plans for the home you choose, and we'll send you our easy-to-use customization request form via e-mail or fax. For just $50, our customization experts will provide an estimate for your requested revisions, and once it's approved, that charge will be applied to your changes. You'll receive either five sets or a reproducible master of your modified design and any other options you select.

BUILDING BASICS

If you want to know more about building techniques—and deal more confidently with your subcontractors—we offer four useful detail sheets. These sheets provide non-plan-specific general information, but are excellent tools that will add to your understanding of Plumbing Details, Electrical Details, Construction Details, and Mechanical Details. These fact-filled sheets will help answer many of your building questions, and help you learn what questions to ask your builder and subcontractors.

HANDS-ON HOME FURNITURE PLANNER

Effectively plan the space in your home using our Hands-On Home Furniture Planner. It's fun and easy—no more moving heavy pieces of furniture to see how the room will go together. The kit includes reusable peel-and-stick furniture templates that fit on a 12"x18" laminated layout board—enough space to lay out every room in your house.

12" X 18" LAMINATED LAYOUT BOARD

THE TOP 10 PLANNING SECRETS

BASICS

ABC

FURNITURE PLANNING SECRETS

FURNITURE PLANNING BASICS

HELPFUL HINTS & SOLUTIONS

OVER 200 FURNITURE TEMPLATES MADE OF REUSABLE CLING VINYL

DECK BLUEPRINT PACKAGE

Many of the homes in this book can be enhanced with a professionally designed Home Planners Deck Plan. Those plans marked with a **D** have a corresponding deck plan, sold separately, which includes a Deck Plan Frontal Sheet, Deck Framing and Floor Plans, Deck Elevations, and a Deck Materials List. A Standard Deck Details Package, also available, provides all the how-to information necessary for building any deck. Get both the Deck Plan and the Standard Deck Details Package for one low price in our Complete Deck Building Package.

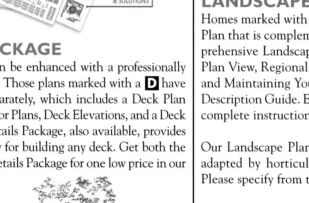

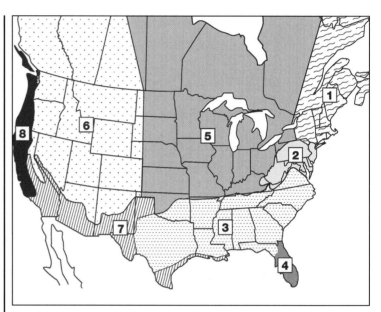

LANDSCAPE BLUEPRINT PACKAGE

Homes marked with an **L** in this book have a front-yard Landscape Plan that is complementary in design to the house plan. These comprehensive Landscape Blueprint Packages include a Frontal Sheet, Plan View, Regionalized Plant & Materials List, a sheet on Planting and Maintaining Your Landscape, Zone Maps, and a Plant Size and Description Guide. Each set of blueprints is a full 18" x 24" with clear, complete instructions in easy-to-read type.

Our Landscape Plans are available with a Plant & Materials List adapted by horticultural experts to eight regions of the country. Please specify from the following regions when ordering your plan:

Region 1: Northeast
Region 2: Mid-Atlantic
Region 3: Deep South
Region 4: Florida & Gulf Coast
Region 5: Midwest
Region 6: Rocky Mountains
Region 7: Southern California & Desert Southwest
Region 8: Northern California & Pacific Northwest

OUR EXCHANGE POLICY

With the exception of reproducible plan orders, we will exchange your entire first order for an equal or greater number of blueprints within our plan collection within **60 days** of the original order. The entire content of your original order must be returned before an exchange will be processed. Please call our customer service department at 1-888-690-1116 for your return authorization number and shipping instructions. If the returned blueprints look used, redlined, or copied, we will not honor your exchange. Fees for exchanging your blueprints are as follows: 20% of the amount of the original order, plus the difference in cost if exchanging for a design in a higher price bracket or less the difference in cost if exchanging for a design in a lower price bracket. (Reproducible blueprints are not exchangeable or refundable.) Please call for current postage and handling prices. Shipping and handling charges are not refundable.

ABOUT REPRODUCIBLES

Reproducibles (often called "vellums") are the most convenient way to order your blueprints. In any building process, you will need multiple copies of your blueprints for your builder, subcontractors, lenders, and the local building department. In addition, you may want or need to make changes to the original design. Such changes should be made only by a licensed architect or engineer. When you purchase reproducibles, you will receive a copyright release letter that allows you to have them altered and copied. You will want to purchase a reproducible plan if you plan to make any changes, whether by using our convenient Customization Program or going to a local architect.

ABOUT REVERSE BLUEPRINTS

Although lettering and dimensions will appear backward, reverses will be a useful aid if you decide to flop the plan. See Price Schedule and Plans Index for pricing.

ARCHITECTURAL AND ENGINEERING SEALS

Some cities and states now require that a licensed architect or engineer review and "seal" a blueprint, or officially approve it, prior to construction. Prior to application for a building permit or the start of actual construction, we strongly advise that you consult your local building official who can tell you if such a review is required.

ABOUT THE DESIGNS

The architects and designers whose work appears in this publication are among America's leading residential designers. Each plan was designed to meet the requirements of a nationally recognized model building code in effect at the time and place the plan was drawn. Because national building codes change from time to time, plans may not fully comply with any such code at the time they are sold to a customer. In addition, building officials may not accept these plans as final construction documents of record as the plans may need to be modified and additional drawings and details added to suit local conditions and requirements. Purchasers should consult a licensed architect or engineer, and their local building official, before starting any construction related to these plans.

LOCAL BUILDING CODES AND ZONING REQUIREMENTS

At the time of creation, these plans are drawn to specifications published by the Building Officials and Code Administrators (BOCA) International, Inc.; the Southern Building Code Congress International, (SBCCI) Inc.; the International Conference of Building Officials (ICBO); or the Council of American Building Officials (CABO). These plans are designed to meet or exceed national building standards. Because of the great differences in geography and climate throughout the United States and Canada, each state, county, and municipality has its own building codes, zone requirements, ordinances, and building regulations. Your plan may need to be modified to comply with local requirements. In addition, you may need to obtain permits or inspections from local governments before and in the course of construction. We authorize the use of the blueprints on the express condition that you consult a local licensed architect or engineer of your choice prior to beginning construction and strictly comply with all local building codes, zoning requirements, and other applicable laws, regulations, ordinances, and requirements. Notice: Plans for homes to be built in Nevada must be redrawn by a Nevada-registered professional. Consult your building official for more information on this subject.

TERMS AND CONDITIONS

These designs are protected under the terms of United States Copyright Law and may not be copied or reproduced in any way, by any means, unless you have purchased reproducibles which clearly indicate your right to copy or reproduce. We authorize the use of your chosen design as an aid in the construction of one single- or multi-family home only. You may not use this design to build a second or multiple dwellings without purchasing another blueprint or blueprints or paying additional design fees.

HOW MANY BLUEPRINTS DO YOU NEED?

Although a four-set building package may satisfy many states, cities, and counties, some plans may require certain changes. For your convenience, we have developed a reproducible plan, which allows you to take advantage of our Customization Program, or to have a local professional modify and make up to 10 copies of your revised plan. As our plans are all copyright protected, with your purchase of the reproducible, we will supply you with a copyright release letter. The number of copies you may need: 1 for owner, 3 for builder, 2 for local building department, and 1-3 sets for your mortgage lender.

DISCLAIMER

The designers we work with have put substantial care and effort into the creation of their blueprints. However, because we cannot provide on-site consultation, supervision, and control over actual construction, and because of the great variance in local building requirements, building practices, and soil, seismic, weather, and other conditions, **WE MAKE NO WARRANTY OF ANY KIND, EXPRESS OR IMPLIED, WITH RESPECT TO THE CONTENT OR USE OF THE BLUEPRINTS, INCLUDING BUT NOT LIMITED TO ANY WARRANTY OF MERCHANTABILITY OR OF FITNESS FOR A PARTICULAR PURPOSE. ITEMS, PRICES, TERMS, AND CONDITIONS ARE SUBJECT TO CHANGE WITHOUT NOTICE.**

IT'S EASY TO ORDER
JUST VISIT
EPLANS.COM
OR CALL
TOLL-FREE
1-800-521-6797

OPEN 24 HOURS, 7 DAYS A WEEK
If we receive your order by 3:00 p.m. EST, Monday-Friday, we'll process it and ship within two business days. When ordering by phone, please have your credit card or check information ready.

CANADIAN CUSTOMERS
Order Toll Free 1-877-223-6389

ONLINE ORDERING
Go to: www.eplans.com

After you have received your order, call our customer service experts at 1-888-690-1116 if you have any questions.

1 BIGGEST & BEST

1001 of our Best-Selling Plans
in One Volume.
1,074 to 7,275 square feet.
704 pgs. $12.95 1K1

2 ONE-STORY

450 designs for all lifestyles.
810 to 5,400 square feet.
448 pgs. $9.95 OS2

3 MORE ONE-STORY

475 Superb One-Level Plans
from 800 to 5,000
square feet.
448 pgs. $9.95 MO2

4 TWO-STORY

450 Best-Selling Designs
for 1½ and 2-stories.
448 pgs. $9.95 TS2

5 VACATION

430 designs for Recreation,
Retirement, and Leisure.
448 pgs. $9.95 VS3

6 HILLSIDE

208 designs for Split-Levels,
Bi-Levels, Multi-Levels,
and Walkouts.
224 pgs. $9.95 HH

7 FARMHOUSE

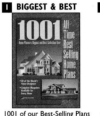

300 fresh designs from
Classic to Modern.
320 pgs. $10.95 FCP

8 COUNTRY HOUSES

208 unique home plans that
combine Traditional Style and
Modern Livability.
224 pgs. $9.95 CN

9 BUDGET-SMART

200 Efficient Plans from
7 Top Designers, that you can
really afford to build!
224 pgs. $8.95 BS

10 BARRIER-FREE

Over 1,700 products and
51 plans for Accessible Living.
128 pgs. $15.95 UH

11 ENCYCLOPEDIA

500 exceptional plans for all
styles and budgets—
The Best Book of its Kind!
528 pgs. $9.95 ENC3

12 SUN COUNTRY

175 Designs from
Coastal Cottages to
Stunning Southwesterns.
192 pgs. $9.95 SUN

13 AFFORDABLE

300 modest plans
for savvy homebuyers.
256 pgs. $9.95 AH2

14 VICTORIAN

210 striking Victorian and
Farmhouse designs from
today's top designers.
224 pgs. $15.95 VDH2

15 ESTATE

Dream big!
Eighteen designers showcase
their biggest and best plans.
224 pgs. $16.95 EDH3

16 LUXURY

170 lavish designs, over 50%
brand-new plans added to a
most elegant collection.
192 pgs. $12.95 LD3

17 WILLIAM E. POOLE

100 classic house plans from
William E. Poole.
224 pgs. $17.95 WP2

18 HUGE SELECTION

650 home plans—
from Cottages to Mansions
464 pgs. $8.95 650

19 SOUTHWEST

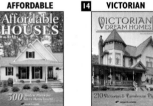

120 designs in Santa Fe,
Spanish, and
Contemporary Styles.
192 pgs. $14.95 SI

20 COUNTRY CLASSICS

130 Best-Selling Home Plans
from Donald A. Gardner.
192 pgs. $17.95 DAG2

21 COTTAGES

245 Delightful retreats from
825 to 3,500 square feet.
256 pgs. $10.95 COOL

22 CONTEMPORARY

The most complete and
imaginative collection of
contemporary designs available.
256 pgs. $10.95 CM2

23 FRENCH COUNTRY

Live every day in the French
countryside using these plans,
landscapes and interiors.
192 pgs. $14.95 PN

24 SOUTHWESTERN

138 designs that capture the
spirit of the Southwest.
144 pgs. $10.95 SW

25 SHINGLE-STYLE

155 home plans from
Classic Colonials to
Breezy Bungalows.
192 pgs. $12.95 SNG

26 NEIGHBORHOOD

170 designs with the feel
of main street America.
192 pgs. $12.95 TND

27 CRAFTSMAN

170 Home plans in the
Craftsman and Bungalow
style. 192 pgs. $12.95 CC

28 GRAND VISTAS

200 Homes with a View.
224 pgs. $10.95 GV

29 MULTI-FAMILY

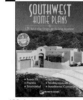

115 Duplex, Multiplex &
Townhome Designs.
128 pgs. $17.95 MFH

30 WATERFRONT

200 designs perfect for your
Waterside Wonderland.
208 pgs. $10.95 WF

Home Planners wants your building experience to be as pleasant and trouble-free as possible.
That's why we've expanded our library of do-it-yourself titles to help you along.

31 NATURAL LIGHT
223 Sunny home plans
for all regions.
240 pgs. $8.95 NA

32 NOSTALGIA
100 Time-Honored
designs updated with
today's features.
224 pgs. $14.95 NOS

33 DREAM HOMES
50 luxury home plans.
Over 300 illustrations.
256 pgs. $19.95 SOD2

34 NARROW-LOT
245 versatile designs
up to 50 feet wide.
256 pgs. $9.95 NL2

35 SMALL HOUSES
Innovative plans for
sensible lifestyles.
224 pgs. $8.95 SM2

36 OUTDOOR
74 easy-to-build designs,
lets you create and build
your own backyard oasis.
128 pgs. $9.95 YG2

37 GARAGES
145 exciting projects from
64 to 1,900 square feet.
160 pgs. $9.95 GG2

38 PLANNER
A Planner for Building or
Remodeling your Home.
318 pgs. $17.95 SCDH

39 HOME BUILDING
Everything you need to know
to work with contractors
and subcontractors.
212 pgs. $14.95 HBP

40 RURAL BUILDING
Everything you need to
know to build your
home in the country.
232 pgs. $14.95 BYC

41 VACATION HOMES
Your complete guide
to building your
vacation home.
224 pgs. $14.95 BYV

42 DECKS
A brand new collection
of 120 beautiful and
practical decks.
144 pgs. $9.95 DP2

43 GARDENS & MORE
225 gardens, landscapes,
decks and more to
enhance every home.
320 pgs. $19.95 GLP

44 EASY-CARE
41 special landscapes
designed for beauty and
low maintenance.
160 pgs. $14.95 ECL

45 BACKYARDS
40 designs focused solely on
creating your own specially
themed backyard oasis.
160 pgs. $14.95 BYL

46 BEDS & BORDERS
40 Professional designs
for do-it-yourselfers.
160 pgs. $14.95 BB

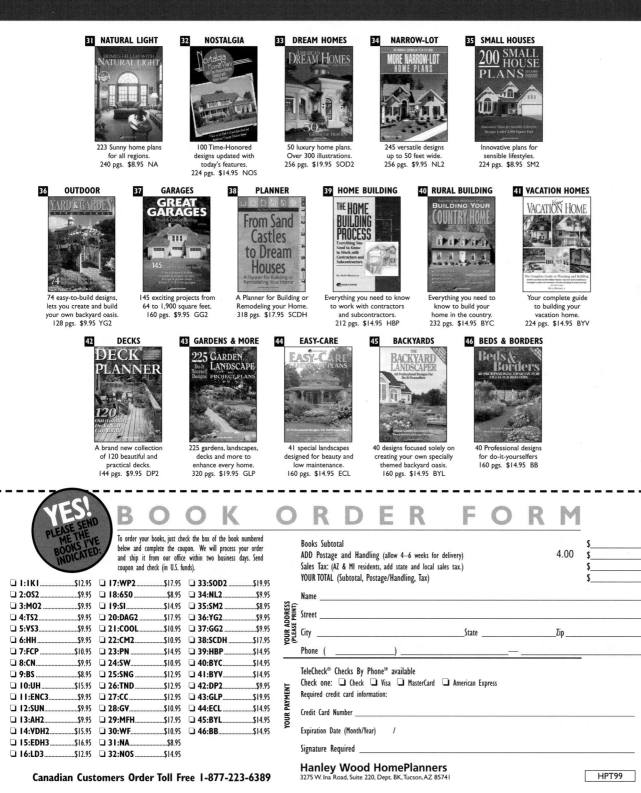

YES! PLEASE SEND ME THE BOOKS I'VE INDICATED:

B O O K   O R D E R   F O R M

To order your books, just check the box of the book numbered below and complete the coupon. We will process your order and ship it from our office within two business days. Send coupon and check (in U.S. funds).

❑ 1:1K1 ....$12.95
❑ 2:OS2 ....$9.95
❑ 3:MO2 ....$9.95
❑ 4:TS2 ....$9.95
❑ 5:VS3 ....$9.95
❑ 6:HH $9.95
❑ 7:FCP $10.95
❑ 8:CN $9.95
❑ 9:BS $8.95
❑ 10:UH $15.95
❑ 11:ENC3 ....$9.95
❑ 12:SUN $9.95
❑ 13:AH2 ....$9.95
❑ 14:VDH2 ....$15.95
❑ 15:EDH3 ....$16.95
❑ 16:LD3 ....$12.95

❑ 17:WP2 ....$17.95
❑ 18:650 ....$8.95
❑ 19:SI $14.95
❑ 20:DAG2 ....$17.95
❑ 21:COOL $10.95
❑ 22:CM2 ....$10.95
❑ 23:PN $14.95
❑ 24:SW $10.95
❑ 25:SNG $12.95
❑ 26:TND $12.95
❑ 27:CC $12.95
❑ 28:GV $10.95
❑ 29:MFH $17.95
❑ 30:WF $10.95
❑ 31:NA $8.95
❑ 32:NOS $14.95

❑ 33:SOD2 ....$19.95
❑ 34:NL2 ....$9.95
❑ 35:SM2 ....$8.95
❑ 36:YG2 ....$9.95
❑ 37:GG2 ....$9.95
❑ 38:SCDH $17.95
❑ 39:HBP $14.95
❑ 40:BYC $14.95
❑ 41:BYV $14.95
❑ 42:DP2 ....$9.95
❑ 43:GLP $19.95
❑ 44:ECL $14.95
❑ 45:BYL $14.95
❑ 46:BB $14.95

Books Subtotal .... $_____
ADD Postage and Handling (allow 4–6 weeks for delivery)   4.00 $_____
Sales Tax: (AZ & MI residents, add state and local sales tax.) $_____
YOUR TOTAL (Subtotal, Postage/Handling, Tax) .... $_____

YOUR ADDRESS (PLEASE PRINT)

Name _____

Street _____

City _____ State _____ Zip _____

Phone (_____) _____ — _____

YOUR PAYMENT

TeleCheck® Checks By Phone™ available

Check one: ❑ Check ❑ Visa ❑ MasterCard ❑ American Express

Required credit card information:

Credit Card Number _____

Expiration Date (Month/Year)   /

Signature Required _____

Canadian Customers Order Toll Free 1-877-223-6389

Hanley Wood HomePlanners
3275 W. Ina Road, Suite 220, Dept. BK, Tucson, AZ 85741

HPT99

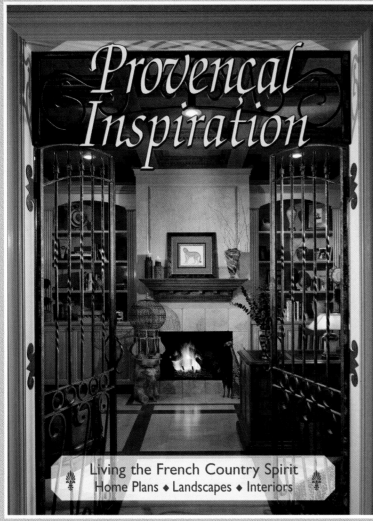
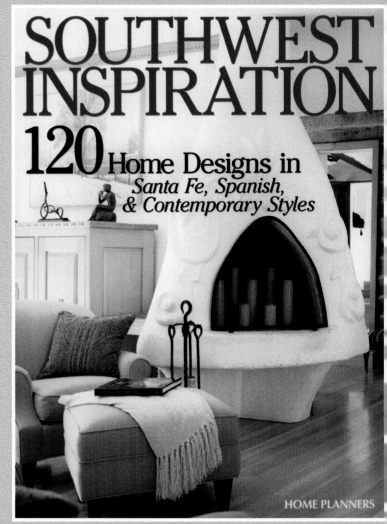